DO NOT BOW DOWN

A WARNING TO THE SAINTS

Althea Lemme

DO NOT BOW DOWN

A WARNING TO THE SAINTS

Althea Lemme

Copyright Page

Do Not Bow Down
Written by: Althea Lemme

Copyright © 2021 by:
All Rights Reserved.

Published by: Rise Publishing Company
ISBN-13: 978-1-7351105-6-1
Printed in the United States of America.

All rights reserved. No part of this publication may be reproduced, stored in a retrieval system, or transmitted in any form or by any means – electronic, mechanical, photocopy, recording, scanning, or otherwise – without the prior written consent of the publisher, except by provided by the United States of America copyright law.

Unless otherwise noted, scripture quotations are taken from the New King James Version®. ©1982 by Thomas Nelson. Used by permission. All rights reserved.

The Holy Bible, 21st Century King James Version® (KJ21®) Copyright ©1994 by Deuel Enterprises, Inc., Gary, SD 57237. All rights reserved.

THE HOLY BIBLE, NEW INTERNATIONAL VERSION®, NIV® Copyright © 1973, 1978, 1984, 2011 by Biblica, Inc.™ Used by permission. All rights reserved worldwide.

Scripture quotations taken from the Amplified® Bible (AMP),
Copyright © 2015 by The Lockman Foundation
Used by permission. www.Lockman.org

Statements use in this book are not said with the intention of harming nor defaming anyone, person, individual, nor thing. All references have been cited and referenced on the Reference Page.

Rise Publishing Company
www.RisePublishingCompany.com

Dedication

First, I want to dedicate this book to the Holy Spirit, who has been my constant friend. Giving honor to Him, The Spirit of wisdom and understanding, the Spirit of counsel and might, the Spirit of knowledge, and the fear of the Lord. Lord, without You, there is no me. Thank You, Heavenly Father (Isaiah 11:2).

Next, I dedicate this book to my Family: my loving Husband, Geoffery Lemme, and my three children, Ashley, Andre, and Sean. I love every one of you. I pray the Lord continues to pour His Spirit on you all and blesses you all continuously.

Finally, to every believer of Jesus Christ, God is looking for His ready bride. God is looking for a people who will honor Him with their whole hearts. The Lord says to you, repent and walk in the freedom that I gave you.

This book is dedicated to you. I pray that as you read the words within this book, you will grow in wisdom and walk in your divine freedom. Receive this reminder and wake-up call. Now is the time to stand firm in Christ and not bow down to the wiles and schemes of the evil one. Shalom.

Contents

Introduction 9

1. In the Beginning 13
2. A Closer Look: Satan's Second Attempt at Worship 23
3. Satan Has Power to Influence Organizations 35
4. Satan Deceives to Gain Worship 53
5. Satan and His Devious Ways 65
6. We Must Stand 73
7. No Compromise 83
8. Love, Not Compromise 95
9. Satan Is an Opportunist 105

Prayer of Deliverance 115

Reference Page 117

Althea Lemme

Introduction

<u>Unveiling the Book</u>

As I sat in my prayer room, awakened by my annoying cell phone alarm, I made my way to the restroom feeling somewhat dazed, and rightly so; the night before, I went to bed relatively late. As I sat there, I was meditating on some scriptures and something else I read that morning that was quite disturbing, to say the least.

That morning, I read that a city council in a particular state subpoenaed the sermons of a few pastors because of comments they made during their sermons concerning, guess what? Homosexuality! Of course, one of the city councilwomen is a lesbian. I recall wanting to see what others said about the issue, so I decided to view the comments. It was the usual. There were so many comments, some slamming Christians and some upholding the same-sex lifestyle. I wanted to post a comment or two but had difficulty doing so.

Do Not Bow Down

My intuition was telling me that God did not want me to post. I tried posting many times but to no avail. Therefore, my interpretation was that God did not want me to share my viewpoints concerning this topic. As I pondered the various comments, I thought about scriptures that might refute some of these comments. Suddenly, I heard loud words ringing from my spirit-man: "BOW DOWN AND WORSHIP ME!" These words reverberated in my spirit.

I do not know how to fully describe it on paper, except it reverberated in my spirit. My spirit discerned that I was hearing the Holy Spirit speaking in my spirit, "BOW DOWN AND WORSHIP ME!" I had no doubt it was the Holy Spirit. I discerned He was allowing me to hear the mind of Satan at the time he tempted Jesus in the wilderness.

Again, I heard the Spirit speaking, and He said, "Throughout history, Satan has placed a demand on Christians and the people of God to bow down and worship him." Immediately, I felt quickened by the Holy Spirit to go to the scriptures where Daniel (Dan. 6:10-14; 3) and the three Hebrew boys were threatened. The king of Babylon, Nebuchadnezzar, set a decree for all to bow down and worship his idol (an image of him) lest they suffer severely and die.

I felt the Holy Spirit wanted me to know that in a similar respect, Christians are being forced to bow down to Satan through the spirit of homosexuality. I must have had a momentary doubt about what I heard because immediately I heard these words that struck the senses in my spirit, "If Satan demanded worship from Jesus, then what makes you think that things are different today?" Then it hit me, and like Jeremiah, I responded out loud, "Aah! Sovereign Lord, You are right. You are right!"

Through this encounter, I know it was the voice of the Holy Spirit who prompted me to write this book. I felt the Lord wanted me to write a small, powerful, and intentional book. I know the Lord wants this book to be a warning to us, His people. It is imperative that we come into agreement with His Word and will, lest we get swept away by our emotions and neglect His warning not to BOW DOWN to any other God except Him!

1

In the Beginning

Throughout biblical history, we learn that Satan's main desire is to be like God (Isa. 14:12). From Genesis to our present time, Satan's foremost desire has always been to be worshipped, and it has not changed. Satan will do anything to achieve his ambitious goal, even if it means challenging God, his Creator. It would be fitting to say that his desire for worship originated in heaven; positionally, this is true. However, Satan's desire to be worshipped began in his heart while he was in heaven, serving as God's anointed cherub.

He was Lucifer, the chief anointed cherub who stood in the very presence of God. He was the one who led the angelic host in worshipping God. He was full of beauty and wisdom. He was beautifully arrayed with gems and had all types of musical instruments built into him. Unfortunately, he was not too keen on the idea of worshipping God any longer. Satan began to see himself just as magnificent, beautiful, wise, and powerful as God.

One day this pompous anointed cherub, Lucifer, decided to abandon his job as the chief worship leader. Lucifer's heart intent was to establish a kingdom for himself. He felt he had enough wisdom, radiance, and clout to have a kingdom of his own where he would be like the Most High God, having power and dominion to rule and reign. Unfortunately, his plans did not work out too well.

For Lucifer to establish his own kingdom, he had to get God, his Creator, out of the way. And we all know nothing, nor anything can withstand the power of God. So a war broke out in heaven, and Lucifer, whose name became Satan (which means "adversary"), found himself cast down out of heaven along with about one-third of the angels who followed him and rebelled against God.

If you are like me, you must have wondered what Satan was thinking challenging his Creator. Did he actually believe he was a match for God? What was worth such humiliation? Was his need for rulership and power worth his defeat?

What Was Lucifer Thinking?

Well, worship, of course! Lucifer was after worship. According to Isaiah 14:1-16, the Spirit of God disclosed what took place in Lucifer's heart. This is what the Spirit said of Lucifer (Isa. 14:12-14 KJV):

> O how thou art fallen from heaven, O Lucifer, son of the morning! How art thou cut down to the ground which did weaken the nations! For thou has said in your heart, "I will ascend into heaven, I will exalt my throne above the stars (angels or sons) of God: I will sit also upon the mount of the congregation, in the sides of the north: I will ascend above the heights of the clouds; I will be like the Most High.

Then we find God disclosing through the prophet Ezekiel, similar utterances of the heart of Lucifer recorded in Ezekiel 28:12-13; 17:

> You were the seal of perfection, full of wisdom and perfect in beauty. You were in Eden, the Garden of God. . . . Your heart was lifted up because of your beauty; you corrupted your wisdom for the sake of your splendor; I cast you to the ground.

So there you have it! Lucifer's motive was to be worshipped just like God. Consequentially, Lucifer and several of the angels found themselves evicted and thrown down to the earth. Of course, things were not the same for them nor the inhabitants of the earth. Shortly after, Lucifer became a rival of God and a deceiver of humanity. And quite fittingly, he became, as I mentioned before, Satan—the adversary. He and the angels who followed him are now demons, though some people still refer to them as fallen angels. We will not argue here nor there because, as you will see later, they will take on many names. The goal here is to establish how this ambitious angel's desire for worship led him to oppose God and sealed his doom for all eternity. But this would not be Satan's last attempt at challenging God's sovereign rule.

Satan's Second Attempt at Dominion and Rulership

Satan's decision to challenge God was his first attempt to secure a kingdom where he could be worshipped; his second attempt was in the Garden of Eden. When God created the earth, He created the Garden of Eden as the home to the first man and his family.

God made two people; I am sure you are no stranger to who they were, a male named Adam and a female named Eve. God gave them total dominion over the earth. Adam and Eve were to procreate, multiply, and have authority over the entire world and everything in it. Adam was the head/husband, and Eve, his wife, was his helper/partner. It was their responsibility to take care of the earth (garden) and have dominion over everything that moves upon it (Gen. 3:15). These people had jobs (see Gen. 2:15 and John 5:17). Do not think you are going to sit up in heaven eating bonbons all day. We will have duties; however, it will not be as laborious as what we do on earth.

Though they had dominion over the earth, I believe Adam and Eve were oblivious to why they were given charge or placed in authority. Among God's many reasons, I believe the Lord put Adam in charge and gave him complete dominion to prevent Satan from taking over the earth and building his kingdom. Remember, Satan desired to have a kingdom where he could be like God and rule and reign.

Because of Genesis 2:16 and 3:5, It is safe to say that although Adam and Eve had dominion over the earth, they did not know good and evil—they had no recognition of it. Therefore, they were oblivious to Satan, his rebellion, fall, and activities on the earth. Initially, they were oblivious to the presence of evil. However, after their encounter and interaction with the serpent (Satan), they became more aware of the difference between good and evil.

Satan, who was now an outcast of heaven, was most likely angry and vexed at the fact that,

A. He failed in his attempt to usurp God's authority;
B. He lost his home in heaven and the glory that came with it; and,
C. God gave these two clay people dominion over the earth, including power and authority over him.

Keep in mind, Adam and Eve possessed something Satan wanted, which was earth. Adam and Eve had a kingdom given to them by God to rule and have dominion over. Earth must have been looking mighty good to Satan. By this time, he did not have a place, Satan was a wanderer, and he certainly could not return to heaven.

I imagine Satan's thoughts must have been, "If I could just take possession of the earth, I could make it my kingdom and rule and reign over it like God. I could have subjects who would worship and serve me." Satan, also known as the devil or deceiver, devised a plan to take dominion and authority from the man and woman God created. The devil knew if he could usurp authority, he would have power over man instead of man having dominion over him. However, Satan is not a fool. Satan realized that the only way he could take control was to get Adam and Eve to doubt God's Word and His instructions concerning the tree in the Garden.

Do Not Bow Down

In the same manner he is doing it today, Satan undermined God's word, His commandment, and gave Adam and Eve a twisted version of God's precepts. He knew if he could scheme to make them distrust God's spoken word, God's authority, including their identity, they would immediately fall into rebellion like him. Once Adam and Eve fell into rebellion, Satan would have the power to entice them to believe his words and act on them. The moment Adam and Eve placed their trust and belief in Satan is when the transference of dominion and authority would occur. Satan knew that if he should reign, he must take control and power away from them—the same concept and notion Lucifer had in his attempt to hijack Heaven.

The devil knew God would not be pleased with Adam and Eve, and as a result, they would be met with a similar fate as him, and it pleased him. Why would Satan be concerned with the treacherous consequences man would face if his goals were to receive worship and destroy God's creation? His eyes were on the prize: Earth and its inhabitants. He wanted a kingdom to rule and reign, and he was going to do anything to accomplish his mission, including deceiving mankind to bow down to him.

Now, how is deception possible? Well, Satan was still a spirit being from the heavenly realm. Earth is made for flesh-and-blood beings. To enter the earth realm, a spirit needs a physical body. This is why and how demons possess or oppress people—by entering their bodies.

Additionally, Jesus needed a physical body during His stay on earth. Spirit beings cannot remain on earth without a physical body. Therefore, Satan, that old devil, sought out an animal that closely related to his nature, a serpent.

Satan's plans went into full effect. He embodied a serpent and was ready to do his deed. What did God say of the serpent he created? He said of all the animals He made, the serpent was the most subtle (Gen. 3:1). The snake was the craftiest, most delicate, and most elusive of all the beasts of the field. There was none like the serpent. Therefore, it was an excellent cover for the devil, the deceiver, and he went into action.

Now both the man and the woman had instructions from God—their Father (Gen. 2:16-17). They could eat of any tree in the Garden except for one tree. The tree in the middle of the Garden of Eden, the Tree of Knowledge of Good and Evil, was off-limits. The consequence of disobeying God's Word and instructions was death. They would not just die but would *surely die*—physically and spiritually.

What does that mean for humankind? It could mean that God meant that they would experience physical death and death beyond the physical body. They would experience the spiritual separation of death. In Satan's attempt to undermine God's word and authority, he told them they would not *really* die, but they would be like God, knowing good and evil. So basically, he told them God lied.

Unfortunately for Adam and Eve, what the devil told them may have initially seemed harmless. Sadly, they both listened to the deceiver's words and his rationale, which was nothing but a twisted version of God's Word.

When Adam and Eve heeded the devil's voice, they were acting in the form of worship. Thus, they bowed their hearts to him and lost dominion and authority over Satan, the earth, and everything in it. Unfortunately, they found out how deadly the devil's words were. Because they fell into Satan's snare, they disobeyed God, rebelled against His Word, and received the death sentence just as God declared (Rom. 6:23). Though Adam and Eve did not experience physical death immediately, they did experience immediate spiritual death. Their sin separated them from God, causing them to be spiritually dead. And like Lucifer, they were separated from God's presence and driven out of the Garden of Eden.

Eventually, both the man and the woman physically died, and so did their offspring. The most devastating aspect was that they were driven from the presence of God. Their fellowship with God shattered. Death, spiritually and physically, were their wages for their sin. According to Roman 6:23, "For the wages of sin is death, but the gift of God is eternal life through Christ Jesus." Sadly, for them and all mankind, the whole world was thrown into an adversarial relationship with God.

Satan's seed—sin—became the carnal nature of man. We needed a miracle to undo the damage. Therein lies the birth of sin and humankind's separation from God. It was the genesis of man's suffering on the earth. It was the beginning of Satan's control over humanity. But praise be to God, who is omniscient and had a backup plan to deliver humankind from sin. That backup plan was a Miracle child JESUS CHRIST, HIS SON! Jesus is the one thing the devil cannot rejoice over. The devil is doomed forever, yet mankind has a second chance to be reborn and reconciled back to God. Hallelujah!

Through God's provision, many have found their way back into fellowship with God through Jesus Christ. However, many, through Satan's lies and deception, are still being led into worshipping him with depraved minds and everything evil.

2

A Closer Look: Satan's Second Attempt at Worship

Now let us talk about Satan's second attempt at power and worship. You might say he already gained power and worship when he usurped it from Adam and Eve; all creation is now under his rule. But let me ask this question: what do we know of the powerful and greedy? You may answer, "They are never satisfied, and they are always thirsty for more and more power." Well, this is true for this diabolical being. Satan gained a foothold into the souls of mankind, and now his mission is to get them to serve him by bowing to his every demand. He wants to do with humanity whatever pleases him. 2 Timothy 2:26 shows that Satan ensnares and takes people captive at will. Satan is a bully. He does not care who you are. All he needs is an opportunity into your life, and he will jump at it.

He wants us to bow down to him, just like Adam and Eve. They yielded to his deception. In like manner, he seduces us using half-truths and a twisted version of God's word. He approaches us like a snake, subtle and clever. But if we are honest, we have all bowed down to him in one form or another. We have all sinned; therefore, we have bowed down to him. If you do not believe, read Romans 3:23 and observe what is taking place in our societies today. Sin is running rampant all over the globe. Man's willful rebellion against God and with help from Satan has corrupted our soul and robbed us of the glory of God.

Satan will not stop until he has the heart and soul of every male, female, child, both born and unborn souls, gay and straight; it does not matter. He works in ways to get unsuspecting men to bow down to him. His primary tools are lies and deception. The essence of Satan is a liar; he hates the truth. He uses deception and lies to turn men's hearts away from the Truth—Jesus Christ. He is a deceiver and a liar; those are his weapons of war; he does not have new tricks. SATAN USES THE SAME OLD TRICKS PLACED INTO NEW BAGS. He may change his tactics, but he will always use lies, deception, or both to get his desired outcome, which is glorification.

Satan's Tactics

Satan uses two tactics, covert and overt tactics. However, his tactics are usually covert. What I mean is that he works undercover. He works behind the scenes; his actions are not detectable, not to the naked eyes nor spiritually undiscerning eyes. He performs this way because lies and deceptions are the means he uses to trap souls into worshipping him even when they are unaware they are doing so. Satan only uses overt tactics when confronted or when his covert activities are exposed, though his attacks are usually covert. That is why Jesus called him the prince of darkness: because all his deeds are done in the dark.

I will attempt to show you a few covert and overt tactics the devil uses to gain worship. Keep in mind that Satan is a powerful being, capable of influencing anyone (except Christ), be it angels, kings, men, and animals. Remember, he convinced about one-third of the angels in heaven to follow him in rebellion against God. Additionally, the deceiver convinced Eve that God lied to them, causing them to rebel against the Creator. So this pompous prince of pride is not a mere powerless being. He can influence men to do depraved things, including deviant sexual acts, the worshipping of self (such as Hollywood stars), and worshipping idols in various forms.

Covert Tactics

A couple of examples of Satan's covert attempts to gain worship are referenced when Ezekiel and Isaiah prophesied to two leaders: the prince of Tyre and the king of Babylon. Some of you, like me, may have wondered or be confused about why I use these passages to identify Satan when they were prophesying to these two leaders. *What does the devil have to do with them?* Well, when you examine the verses closely, you will discover in both prophecies that

God was addressing these two pompous kings and Satan simultaneously. God reminded Satan of his pride, rebellion, and consequences resulting from his prideful heart toward the Most High. Let us look at the passages again.

In Ezekiel 28:12-17 (AMP), God told the prophet, Ezekiel:

Take up a lamentation (funeral poem to be sung) for the king of Tyre, and say unto him, "Thus says the Lord God. You had the full measure of perfection and finishing touch full of wisdom and perfect in beauty. You were in Eden, the garden of God: every precious stone was your covering . . . they were prepared on the day you were created. You were the anointed cherub who covers and protects, and I placed you there. You were on the holy mountain of God; you walked in the midst of the stones of fire (sparkling jewels). You were blameless in your ways from the day you were created until unrighteousness and evil was found in you. Through the abundance of your commerce, you were internally filled with lawlessness and violence, and you sinned; therefore, I cast you as a profane and unholy thing from the mountain of God. I have destroyed you, O covering cherub from the midst of the stones of fire. Your heart was proud and arrogant because of your beauty; you destroyed your wisdom for the sake of your splendor. I cast you to the ground; I lay you before kings that they may look at you."

These scriptures highlight Satan's death sentence; it is no wonder God told Ezekiel to take up a funeral poem.

Now let us look at Isaiah 14:12-14 (KJV):

God told Isaiah to take up a proverb against the King of Babylon. "How are thou fallen from heaven, O Lucifer, son of the morning! How art thou cut down to the ground, which didst weaken the nations! For thou has said in thine heart, I will ascend into heaven, I will exalt my throne above the stars of God: I will sit also upon the mount of the congregation in the sides of the north: I will ascend above the heights of the clouds; I will be like the most High."

Now, as you read these two passages, you may have noticed that God was speaking through these prophets to address two leaders whose hearts were filled with pride. However, take note that both were under the influence of Lucifer. They were displaying the same characteristics and nature as Lucifer. Therefore, God pronounced judgment upon them.

Going back to what I mentioned earlier, Satan's mission to be elevated caused him to influence these kings, whether through possession or influencing their minds. Satan knew how to work covertly through these leaders. Yet God, who is omniscient, brought judgment on both leaders and Satan simultaneously. Now, if you do not think God can address the kings and Satan simultaneously, I implore you to read the incident with Jesus and Simon Peter found in Mark 8:33. Jesus rebuked Satan, who spoke through Peter against the plans of God. It was Peter's voice, but it was Satan's mind that spoke. Remember, Jesus said, "Get behind me, Satan," while looking at Peter.

Here are the points: Satan works covertly to secure worship for himself, and it does not matter how he achieves his goals. He wants to be exalted and worshipped like the Most High. Thus, Satan hides his presence and activities, so he cannot be detected.

Overt Tactics

Satan will only reveal his identity when he is detected and forced or when summoned, whether directly or indirectly, as it was with Jesus' fasting. Jesus' fast alerted the spirit realm. For example, in Satan's quest for worship, this brazen, prideful, fallen angel showed up at the end of Jesus' fast in an attempt to get the Son of God to bow down and worship him. During this encounter, Satan did not hide his identity and, interestingly enough, did not seemed like he needed to. Obviously, the two knew each other. Jesus and Satan came face-to-face for the first time since Jesus left the throne of heaven. A great spiritual battle was about to take place. Satan knew that Jesus was in a physically weakened state because he had been fasting for forty days and nights. This was an opportunity to take advantage of the God-Man. "After all, how powerful could he be now that he is in human form?" Satan must have thought. "I will deceive him into worshipping me."

We read in the Gospels how Satan went after Jesus, the Son of God, to get Him, his Creator, to bow down to Him. I guess it did not work in heaven, so he was going to attempt to get the God-Man to bow to him now that God was in human flesh. He probably thought, "Well, it worked with Adam and Eve, so why not?" He was able to deceive Adam and Eve and gain possession of the earth, so if he could get the Son of God to bow down to him, then he would be *like* God.

He would not *be* God because Satan could never be God, but he would share in His reign, and that is what he wanted.

If you are familiar with the Bible, you may already know how this went down. After Jesus' baptism, scripture says the Spirit drove Jesus into the wilderness to be tempted by the devil. The devil tempted and harassed the Lord after His fast in the wilderness. Satan hoped to trick Jesus to obey his words just as he beguiled Adam and Eve in the Garden. The story is recorded in the Gospels of Luke and Matthew, both in chapter 4. However, I prefer Matthew's version because I believe Matthew gave the proper sequence of the temptation. See, the devil does not want to be seen doing his dirty works; he prefers to work undercover in darkness. Satan is very calculated and is not going to show you his intent. He wants you to think it is about you, when in fact, it is about him and what he desires, which is power, dominance, and worship. He will not just come to you and outright tell you or demand you to worship him; no, he must do it subtly. As I said, he will make it about you and your rights, and sadly, he will tell you it is what God wants for you.

Matthew records that after Jesus' forty-day fast, Jesus was extremely hungry. The tempter, the devil, went full force with his temptations. First, he tried to get Jesus to turn the stones into bread. Quite frankly, the devil played a clever move because Jesus was completing or completed his fast. How convenient! Jesus was hungry. Jesus is the Son of God. *Or is he? Why not prove it?* Turn these stones into bread. Notice it is the temptation of food – the desire of the flesh, that Satan used to bait the first man to sin. The flesh – the appetite with which he tempted Adam and Eve – he now is attempting to use on Jesus. Indeed we are the weakest, especially after a fast. You know how that is. Some of us cannot even handle one day of fasting; afterward, we want to eat everything in sight.

Anyway, the devil's tactic was to have Jesus prove his identity that He, meaning Jesus, was indeed the Son of God. Therefore, Satan enticed Him by saying, *"If* you are the Son of God, turn these stones into bread. However, Jesus did not have to prove anything. Jesus pulled out the word of God (the SWORD) and pierced him with, "Man shall not live by bread alone but on every word that comes from God's mouth." Essentially, Jesus told the devil, "I am not going to listen to you nor my flesh" (Matt. 4:4).

When Satan noticed that his antics backfired, he tried to convince Jesus to jump off a cliff. Maybe he wanted Jesus to commit suicide, yet I think it was more about Jesus obeying him. Of course, God would have delivered His Son, but at what cost? The cost of humanity, of course. Coincidently enough, Satan used the same response on Jesus with the hopes of creating doubt, but this time, Satan applied God's Word to legitimize his request.

Satan's tactic was to continue to create doubt in Jesus' mind concerning his identity in hopes that Jesus would obey his word. He basically used covert tactics to obtain worship, but when those ploys failed, he went straight to an overt approach. According to Matthew, the devil took Jesus up on a high mountain and showed him all the kingdoms of the world and offered them to Jesus, saying, "All these I will give to you if you will BOW DOWN AND WORSHIP ME." Satan moved from a covert to an overt approach. He was not getting anywhere with Jesus, for the Lord withstood him with the written

Word. That old devil was feeling the blows of the sword, so to save himself, he went for the jugular.

Interestingly the devil did not hide his identity from Jesus; Jesus knew that the temptations were coming from the devil. The temptations were strong. However, Jesus, knowing the source of them, fought back with the truth of God's word and defeated the devil.

As Christians, we must be like Jesus. We must recognize the areas the devil operates in, even within our own lives. We must learn the ways and venues he uses to entice us to bow down to him. As with Jesus, the devil will use various methods to see which method will work and which methods we are most susceptible to. Satan wants to know which one of his attacks we will fall for and how he can attack us without being detected. He is the master of working undercover most times without being detected.

Satan's Deceptive Snares

As with the temptation of Jesus in the wilderness, the devil will use different methods or test other techniques to see which ones we will fall prey to and how he can seduce us without detection. This is the same manner in which Satan works in our world today and causes chaos everywhere. And if I can be honest, the world is partly under his influence right now. There are all forms of evil and ungodly behaviors, perversions and wickedness, divisiveness, and hatred spewing forth. Unfortunately, many who are unaware of him and his activities are blaming God. And that is what he wants people to do, blame God so they can turn away from God and turn to him, whether by their own free will or by his force.

This diabolical prideful being is a master at undermining God's love toward man. He causes chaos in people's lives and influences men to blame God. Satan's deflective tactic is precisely what happened in the Garden of Eden. Satan undermined God's love for Adam and Eve, made them believe that God's love was insufficient to sustain them, and tricked them into thinking God was holding out on them. Satan convinced Adam and Eve that they were not complete: they had missed out on being like God. Remember, God created them in His image and likeness; what an honor it was and still is. Yet, Satan convinced them that it was not enough—they, too, could be like God. What deception!

And who better to show them how to attain the height of godhood than him, the devil? (I am being facetious here). Even though he was (and still is) a convicted felon on the loose, he was going around deceiving people that he could improve their lives. He could make them stars, give them power, fame, money, love, etc. Here, in the Garden of Eden, he provided counsel on achieving new heights. He is still giving counsel through "enlightened" celebrities, false teachers, false prophets, fake pastors, greedy politicians, and the like. Yet he will not disclose who he is nor reveal his mission—of course not!

As I mentioned earlier, it appeared that both Adam and Eve did not know it was the fallen Lucifer who was speaking to them. Eve thought it was the serpent. It makes one wonder if Adam and Eve were able to communicate with animals. Why would Eve talk to a snake if they could not converse? Imagine doing that today. And why would Satan disguise himself in the form of a snake? Remember, God said the snake was the most cunning and most subtle of all his creatures. Hmm . . . Satan hid in the snake or disguised himself as a snake. That is the epitome of deception.

It is no different than what we are experiencing in our culture today. We have snakes, serpents, and vipers who disguise themselves to deceive and lure people away from God's Word and His way. Leviathan, that twisted serpent, is very much at work in our cultures now more than ever, twisting the truth, twisting the word of God, twisting and turning, making light to appear as dark and dark to appear as light. Calling blindness sight and sight blindness

Just imagine someone coming to you disguised as someone else with the intent of deceiving you. That would make your blood boil, would it not? This is what the deceiver is doing in our culture today. Satan has disguised himself as an angel of light; so have his messengers, his demons. Satan camouflages himself to deceive many into listening and heeding to his voice. He operates undercover, making light dark, and dark light. That is his snakish nature, very subtle, very crafty.

His mission is to secure worship for himself while destroying many souls. He not only wants worship, but he also wants to destroy people, even the very ones who serve and defend him. Jesus told us through the Gospel that Satan is a thief who comes only to steal, kill, and destroy. He will stop at nothing to make slaves out of humankind, which stems from his hatred for God and His creations. So far, we have learned that Satan has managed to invade a serpent, influence

Do Not Bow Down

angels, hide behind idols, and possess kings. Satan even attempted to get the Son of God to bow down to him. What more do you think he will try?

3
Satan Has Power to Influence Organizations

<u>Understanding the Spiritual</u>

I asked the question, "Who or what is influencing our cultures and our societies today?" When I look around, I see things being done, I hear things being said, and it blows my mind. My mind cannot, in its natural state, fathom the things that I am witnessing; I am sure I am not the only one. The only way to comprehend is through a biblical viewpoint. Understanding that the world is under the influence of Satan takes revelation given by the Holy Spirit. My natural interpretations without the Holy Spirit would have left me in utter confusion and despair; I assume it is the same for you — the reader.

This confusion is truly justified because the natural man (the unregenerate person) cannot understand the things of God. After all, such things are spiritually discerned. It is the Spirit of God that helps us understand spiritual things, both evil and good. Without the Spirit of revelation, truth, and knowledge, we as believers would be at a loss.

Sadly, many believers are lost. We have not seen things through authentic biblical lenses because we have been deceived. "How so?" You ask? Well, when we observe things that are happening in our cultures, witnessing corruption, seeing evil, and denying the fact that the devil is behind all or most corruption and exempting the devil from being the cause, then we have become deceived by the devil. I understand, no Christian likes to believe that Satan can deceive them, but in my opinion, that is a dangerous stance. I am not saying that man's heart is not deceitfully wicked and cannot devise great evil, but we should not make the mistake of thinking Satan is totally hands-off. And we Christians should not be arrogant, prideful, nor oblivious to the fact that Satan can deceive Christians; on the contrary, we are not exempt; we are the devil's targets. And truly, at this very moment, as I am writing, many Christians are being deceived.

Are You Being Deceived?

How does a deceived Christian look? A deceived Christian is a person who has confessed Christ as Lord and Savior, yet their profession does not align with their actions. A deceived Christian is always learning but never able to come to the knowledge of the truth (2 Tim 3:7, NIV). For example, a deceived Christian may spend many years attending various Bible studies, prayer services, or church services yet will argue the validity of homosexuality, abortion, fornication, etc. However, those acts are condemned in scripture. Basically, a deceived Christian joins the world, calling light darkness, and darkness light. They are the ones who walk with God while holding hands with the devil and ignoring the consequences. A deceived Christian disregards the warning in Romans 12:2; they are conformed to this world and have not renewed their minds to become transformed into the image of Jesus Christ.

Do not become arrogant and prideful, thinking that as a Christian, you and I cannot become deceived or influenced by the enemy. Having that attitude is the surest way to be deceived by him. The devil wants to possess you, take ownership over your mind, and influence you. Satan desires to affect your character, your spiritual development, and your behavior. Satan can exert his influence without changing the underlying values and motivation. The devil may not be able to change your religious beliefs or your motivation to do good, but he can influence you to carry his plans by employing a religious spirit. Therefore, be humble!

Dismantling Ignorant and Religious Beliefs

Additionally, many believe that the devil has no power and cannot influence a Christian because they are saved. Others believe if they acknowledge that Satan has any kind of power, they are saying that his power is equivalent to God's power. However, anyone who holds those beliefs are relatively ignorant. You should not hold on to such a mindset. As believers, we ought to know that Satan's power is no match for God's omnipotent power. God is the only El Elyon; God is Almighty. He has no equal.

The truth is, in spite of religious beliefs, Satan reserved a measure of power after his fall. If he did not possess a fraction of his power, God would not have warned His children. God warns us through the scriptures by instructing us to put on the whole armor of God so we can withstand the devil's wiles. What are wiles? According to lexico.com, wiles are devious or cunning stratagems employed in manipulating or persuading someone to do what one wants. Come on, who does that sound like? We must wake up and pay attention. Yes, Satan has some dangerous arsenals, so we must not be ignorant of his plots and schemes.

Unfortunately, many believers have fallen prey. They believe Satan lost his power at the cross. In actuality, Satan has lost his dominion and authority over mankind, not his ability to influence, deceive, and destroy — he is still doing that. God will revoke the remainder of Satan's power at the final judgment. On that day, he will be stripped and thrown into the lake of fire — his final destination.

In the meantime, he can control and influence humanity. If you are not convinced and still want proof, just look around you. You do not need discernment to detect his paw prints all over the world. Christian believers must be aware! To prevent falling under Satan's influence, one must follow and trust in the scripture of our Holy God and not lean on our own understanding.

Stand on the Word of God

Leaning on your understanding is sending an aroma to the devil while inviting him for dinner. Satan is a roaring lion seeking whom he may devour; resist him steadfast in the faith as you lean on the Word of God (1 Pet. 5:8-9).

You must stand on the Word of God because this roaring lion only has power over those who have not recognized that Jesus' death, burial, resurrection, ascension, and glorification have defeated the devil. When Jesus defeated Satan at the cross, He took dominion and authority away from him and reconciled man to their authority and dominion through Him, Christ Jesus. As a result, our confession of Jesus Christ gives us God's power and authority over Satan and his demons.

Reclaimed Power and Authority

Because of Jesus' ascension and victory, we have reclaimed the power to influence. Therefore, we must not allow Satan to entice our lives; he is cunning and will swiftly act when given the opportunity. The devil and his demons are subjected to believers because Jesus returned the power and authority to man. The same power and authority Satan stole from Adam and Eve in the Garden of Eden has returned.

However, if a believer refuses to accept this truth and holds on to misconceived notions, believing that Satan does not have power nor influence, then that believer may very well be a pawn the devil wants to use to carry out his diabolical schemes. Do not fall prey to believing Satan is powerless.

Influence to Gain Worship

The question that should be on the table is, how can Satan influence people, especially believers, and get them to worship him? It is no secret how Satan accomplishes his goals. Therefore, let us look at a few examples from the Old Testament, and then we will look at some examples from the New Testament.

Earlier, I referenced Ezekiel 28 and Isaiah 14 and stated that Satan was cast down to earth for his sin of rebellion. However, it is essential to note that he did not act alone. In his craftiness, Satan convinced a significant number of angels to rebel with him; to be exact, a third of the angels rebelled against God.

Just to make it clear, Satan convinced one-third of an innumerable host of angels to follow him in rebellion. To be precise, Job 38:7 calls the angels stars and sons of God. Imagine that? These heavenly hosts, who God adorned, were influenced by Satan. WOW. Was it his rank? His leadership style? His charm, his beauty, his splendor? Or was it his wisdom? What was it about Satan that persuaded these angels to follow him? No one but the Almighty God knows.

However, according to scripture, Satan was the anointed cherub who was full of wisdom and beauty. Could this the anointed cherub be the prince angel in charge of worship? Were angels a part of his administration of ministering to God? Perhaps, as their prince, they were seduced by his grand scheme of a kingdom, where they, too, could be like God, having wisdom, knowledge, power, glory, and honor. He must have persuaded them that they would no longer have to listen to God nor carry out His biddings. Satan must have insinuated that these angels could make their own decisions. He must have appealed to their identity or lack thereof, promising them independence and power over their own lives, topped with an extravagant lifestyle more glorious than the one they had with the Almighty.

Nonetheless, I am only speculating. Remember, this was how Satan seduced Eve and employed the same attempt with our Savior. He appealed to their identity, telling them that they could be like God—though they were already like God, made in God's image and likeness. Jesus himself was God incarnate. Yet Satan attempted and succeeded in one case to influence them to disobey God. In Adam and Eve's case, Satan promised them independence from God and that they could know what was good and evil on their terms. Notice how everyone has their truths or determines their own truth these days? It is not new, and it started in the Garden of Eden. Undoubtedly, Satan utilized great persuasion methods, especially having convinced one-third of the angels to leave their abode to join him in his rebellion against God.

If Satan possessed the clout to convince millions of angelic hosts to rebel with him, then how much more impressionable are we? We are not created like the angels; we do not have their same great strength and power. We depend on God; we need His strength and power. God created angels with power and strength because they are ordained to carry out God's assignments and duties in the spiritual realm. The point here is to remind ourselves that the same power and influence Satan used to influence and enticed millions of angels away from worshipping God is the same power and influence he is using on us today.

Pride Is a Spirit

Let us look at some more examples of how Satan can influence the children of God. King David, a worshipper and the king God called "a man after His own heart," was tempted and manipulated by the devil. 1 Chronicles 21 drops a bomb by stating, Satan moved (or influenced) David to number or take a census of Israel's army. God was tremendously displeased with David's actions.

I believe Satan influenced David through his mind, precisely pride. The scripture did not specify, but I suspect David was feeling proud of his militant army. I believe David forgot that it was not the strength of man but the arm of the Lord that fought for him and brought many victories. Perhaps that day, David was feeling down and needed to cheer himself up. Maybe he was feeling a bit inferior, and he could have been emotional. Or, perhaps, for that brief moment, Satan or his demons were monitoring David's every move.

Could it be that the devil and his minions were listening to David's every word, listening, watching for a moment of weakness? I dare to say emphatically yes. Wasn't that the case with Peter when Satan requested to sift Simon Peter like wheat? (Luke 22:31). Peter was a man with a few weaknesses, pride being one of them. No telling what would have become of Peter if the Lord had not prayed for him. Indeed, the spirit of pride hung around, waiting like a roaring lion on the hunt for its prey. I am sure Satan was waiting for the perfect opportunity to lunge at King David.

I believe the king may have been reflecting on his remarkable achievements in warfare. No doubt, there was a door open to allow the spirit of pride to enter. Satan is that spirit of pride or the master spirit of pride. He managed to get David to bow down to his influence, which could have killed him if God had not made a covenant with his fathers. The scripture tells us that Satan moved David to take a census of Israel, a thing that greatly displeased God, so much so that it cost David seventy thousand men.

Perhaps you, too, have experienced pride in your own life and even now may be struggling with that spirit. Pride can take the form of boasting, thinking of yourself more highly than you ought to, or believing your strength produced your achievements and accomplishments. Perhaps you are a supporter or involved in a group, an organization, or causes that have the spirit of pride and exalts themselves against the knowledge of God. Please understand that the spirit reveals the need and desire to be worshipped. The number one goal of pride is to be high and lifted up, exalted high above the Most High's throne. Its agenda is to get you to worship and serve it. It is also there to influence your decisions and affection for God. Whatever the case may be, David was a man of prayer, yet he was not immune from being influenced by the spirit of pride, and neither are we.

What am I saying? I am saying Satan can and will influence us through our pride if we do not submit ourselves to God. He looks for our weaknesses. Let us remember that PRIDE is a catalyst for wrecking our relationship with God. It is one of the seven deadly sins God hates—a proud look. Pride, at times, can trigger a swift judgment from the Lord or cause you to self-destruct. Pride is a tremendous doorway for Satan to gain a foothold in our lives so he could influence our thoughts and actions. Pride is a bridge to the demonic world, and rightly so, that bridge was constructed by Lucifer (Satan). It is a bridge the devil entices his victims to pursue. As you may have already known or just are beginning to learn, pride is not limited to individuals but involves movements, organizations, and causes.

As you will hopefully see more clearly in this book, pride is a spirit you cannot see with natural eyes, but you can see its manifestations. It has a plan: to exalt itself against the knowledge of God, to dominate our culture, and to bring men, women, children, churches, and governments under its rule. Pride takes on different faces, but it is one spirit, and it feeds off worship. The LGBTQ organization is one of the many faces of PRIDE. It says, "Bow down and worship me."

Rank, Position, and Power

Another biblical example of Satan's influence is in Job 1:12-17. Satan influenced the Chaldean and Sabean bands to kill Job's servants and steal his camels, oxen, and asses. How do we know that Satan had anything to do with the murdering of Job's servants? Well, it is right there in print. Satan declared an all-out war on Job's entire household, including his servants. Satan sought to tempt Job, and God allowed it. Under the limitations and provisions set by God, Satan had the power to do to Job as he willed.

So you see, though Satan could not influence Job directly, he influenced wicked men to achieve his demonic oppression toward Job. His influence over the evil men was a tactic he employed to destroy Job's livelihood. Satan's chief goal was to gain Job's heart, which would have caused Job to reject God. Think about it: Satan may not influence you directly, but he can use wicked people to do evil to you and your family, friends, race, etc. Satan utilizes many tactics with the intention of turning you away from God while leaving you vulnerable to his influence.

What about king David's son, Solomon? Satan used his strange wives to draw his heart away from God. King Solomon was the wisest king that ever lived, yet the sin of lust (inherited from David, his father) led him to take many wives and concubines from amongst the heathen nations. Solomon built his wives temples so they could worship their gods or idols. His wives were idolaters or, in other words, devil worshippers, who eventually turned Solomon's heart away from serving God.

These strange women seduced Solomon into serving their idols or gods. They lured him into building altars or shrines. These altars or shrines most likely held replicas of devils.

You may say Satan had nothing to do with Solomon moving away from God, and in one sense, you are right. It was the lust of his flesh. Solomon lusted after these strange women. However, is it possible that it was Satan's plan? Could it be that Satan was aware of Solomon's issue with lust and used these women to lure the king to sin against God? I believe so. Why? Because these women were not godly women of Israel; they were pagan women, and Solomon had the sin of lust in his bloodline.

Now, what was it about these pagan women that drew him to them? Witchcraft! I believe these women were in the practice of casting all types of spells, witchcraft, etc. Most likely, some of their practices may have been toward the king. And, of course, those practices are from the kingdom of darkness. Witchcraft and all forms of sorcery can affect people's lives, governments, families, etc. Some of you may have witnessed the chaos taking place in our nation right now.

In the year 2020, we experienced the craziest year for the US election. Did you know there were witches and wiccans—people involved in witchcraft—who went to the White House to cast spells and deploy demonic spirits against the president and his administration? The goal of those who were operating in witchcraft was to create an upset and uproar concerning the 2020 election. Did they succeed? Well, time will tell.

Overall, Solomon was influenced indirectly by Satan through his pagan wives. They managed to bring Solomon to his knees before idols. Satan utilized Solomon's pagan wives as arsenals against him. His actions, like Adam and Eve, were acts of rebellion against God's Word. His efforts greatly affected his ability to sustain rulership over his kingdom and his family. Did Satan have a plan for Solomon? Of course, he did! His goal is always about destruction and gaining worship. Satan wanted to destroy Solomon by turning his heart away from serving God, with hopes that Solomon would worship him instead. Satan used these strange women as bait so they could induce Solomon's heart to rebel against God.

Because God endowed His servants with prophetic words, visions, and insight, Satan knew there was a coming Promise and discerned the coming Messiah's lineage. Therefore, Satan's number one tactic and goal was to destroy David's seed. The devil knew that if he could seduce Solomon's heart, then he could impact the coming Messiah, which could have divided and destroyed Israel.

Was Solomon aware that these women were influencing him? Probably not, or maybe not at first. After all, perhaps they were beautiful women. And at first, he probably thought he had a strong faith in God after hearing from God before. But the more he associated with these women, the deeper into sin he got, until one day he may have found himself addicted to all forms of sexual immorality, idolatry, witchcraft, and everything associated with what his wives were entangled with at that time. Isn't that the case with many of us even today? We find ourselves lured into things, whether by invitation, lust, curiosity, or even to fulfill some emotional need produced by emotions such as anger or fear.

Let Us Evaluate Our Involvement

It is time for me to ask you a heart-provoking question, and I want you to seriously think about your answer and take inventory of your involvement. What replica, idol, movement, cause, organization, or idea is Satan using to influence you? Is Satan inducing your home, your church congregation, or the organization or movement to which you belong? Have you considered what replica or idol Satan is hiding behind exerting influence? Have you joined your heart with any of them, as King Solomon did with his strange wives?

You must consider these questions. We have too many movements and organizations that are involved in pagan practices. Some movements and organizations focus on believers with the intent to exert influence, hoping we will turn away from worshipping God. It is the devil's agenda to turn us away from our devotion to God and become devil worshippers.

Admittedly, that is not all Satan will do. Satan wants to destroy those who are a threat to his kingdom. His mission is to steal, kill, and destroy (John 10:10). I will later provide proof of women like Solomon's wives in our present culture using ancient demonic practices to influence various areas of our cultures and societies, including families and government.

Now let us look at some New Testament examples. Do you recall how Satan influenced Peter in Mark 8:33 to rebuke Jesus? *How was Satan able to influence if Peter was walking closely with Jesus?* When you read the passage, you will see that Satan was able to control some areas of Peter's life, and because of that, I believe he was able to use Peter's mind and mouth to speak against God's plan. It was Peter's mind that Satan influenced. It was Peter's voice that spoke, but it was Satan's mind. Which means Satan had access to Peter's soul. And because of that access, Peter had difficulty controlling those areas. Therefore, I believe there was a possibility that Satan hijacked Peter's personality, which means Peter did not fully surrender his heart to the Lord. He may have had areas in his life that were not submitted to Christ, thus giving Satan access to influence him.

Jesus recognized the hijacking, so Jesus rebuked Satan and not Peter. Jesus knew Satan influenced Peter's mind and thoughts. If Satan can influence Peter's mind, no doubt he can do the same to us if we are not yielded to God.

Open Doors and Footholds

Recall what I said about the spirit of pride? Well, Peter had an issue with pride, along with other things; therefore, Satan gained a foothold in him. How else could he influence Peter? Peter was walking with Jesus daily; he was privy to the things of the Kingdom, yet Satan sought to buffet him or, in Jesus' words, "to sift him as wheat" (Luke 22:31). Thank God Jesus prayed for him. Satan was trying to use Peter to stop God's plan.

What about Judas, another disciple of Jesus, the one who betrayed him? Was Satan not able to influence him too? Satan wooed Judas, and Judas also seemed to be possessed by him. Though Judas walked with Jesus and was one of the twelve disciples, Judas had areas of his soul that were open for Satan to come in and out of as he chose. Satan had footholds in Judas. Scripture said Satan entered Judas at the Last Supper and moved him to betray his Lord (John 13:27).

I shared these examples to show how nothing has changed. Satan had the power to influence those from the biblical days, and Satan retains the same capabilities to compel men today.

You may say, "I am filled with the Holy Ghost." Look, some of you might agree or disagree, but King David was filled with the Holy Spirit, King Saul was filled with the Holy Spirit, and they were both influenced by Satan. If we open ourselves up to evil, then evil will come in. God would not instruct us to put on His whole armor if we were immune to Satan's influences. Scripture tells us that we do not fight against flesh-and-blood, but we fight against unseen powers of darkness.

We should never underestimate the devil's power to influence. Jesus called Satan a thief whose mission is to steal, kill, and destroy; it does not matter who you are. Solomon was the wisest man to live; the Bible said that. This wise man who wrote both Proverbs and Ecclesiastics was drawn into idolatry by seducing spirits or devils. Peter walked with Jesus, and the devil influenced him. David, a worshipper, a man after God's own heart, was influenced by Satan. Satan moved an army of bandits to kill Job's servants and took his camels. Do not forget the numerous angels he convinced to follow him in rebellion against their Creator!

Yes, Satan is a formidable foe, and we should not overlook his power. He influences people, military forces, kings, governments, leaders, and even churches etc. Yet, despite how influential Satan can be, he is limited in what he can do. God has placed Satan on a leash, so to speak (Job 37).

Satan is still exercising his power and authority on the earth but illegally. I say illegally because according to Colossians 2:15, by way of the Cross, Jesus disarmed principalities and powers, making them a public spectacle. Also, Ephesians 4:10 said Jesus ascended above **all** heavens that he might fulfill all things. So the devil, the serpent, that ancient dragon, is defanged. However, many believers are not aware of this truth. To be honest, I believe this oblivion is the call for why Satan and his demons still have power over them.

We Must Discern

Christians operate as though they do not know we have reclaimed all power and authority. Many are still living under the control and influence of the devil. It seems like they live under his control or at least are influenced by him today more than ever because they have bought into his lies and deceptions. And not to mention, many choose the lies of the devil by abstaining from exercising their God-given authority and not utilizing their spiritual gifts. For example, if we exercise our gift of discernment, then we can discern between good and evil spirits.

We need to know what is of the Holy Spirit and what is of the devil. We need to know what spirit we attach ourselves to when we affiliate with certain groups, organizations, causes, political parties, etc.

Due to the lack of spiritual discernment, I see many believers allowing themselves to be deceived and taken captive at will by the devil. They have opened themselves up to demonic influences by joining forces with the world and world systems. Many are bowing down via agreement to these evil world forces that are under the influence of Satan. They have given ears to none other than the powers that be. What are those powers that be? I listed a few earlier, but I will mention them again: government, politics, education, health care, the entertainment industry, movements, causes, and the like.

It seems like the devil established many idols and many altars in his efforts to entrap believers to bow down to him. Here is an example. My daughter told me of a situation where a child was taken to a health care place; the child's mother wanted the receptionist to refer to the daughter as "it." Her mother did not want anyone using pronouns that refer to her specific gender because the girl did not like her God-given sex. The girl was only twelve years old.

Do Not Bow Down

Now, if, as believers, we were to find ourselves in that situation, how should we react? Should we comply, bow down? Standing before our eyes is a female who prefers the pronoun "it." We may follow suit and, just as the receptionist, call the girl by her name. But do you see the trap? It is easy to say, "Well, I am just going to comply because I do not want to offend anyone nor cause an issue." However, we must take a stand! We must open our mouths and explicitly say, "I am not going to bow down to this nonsense."

4

Satan Deceives to Gain Worship

Satan deceives people into indirectly worshipping him by hiding his identity. Previously I gave some examples of how Satan brought great kings down to ordinary people who heeded his unctions. He manipulates the thoughts and actions of people and groups to fulfill his desire for worship. Therefore, as believers, we must put on the whole armor of God, from the helmet of salvation down to the sandal of peace (Eph. 6). Along with the armor of God, we need the Spirit of discernment and the Spirit of wisdom. We must have wisdom, and we must ask God for it because many of us Christians have a lot of knowledge but lack the wisdom to apply the knowledge God has given us. True wisdom and understanding come from the Word of God.

Do Not Bow Down

Jesus told us to be as shrewd as serpents and wise as doves (Matt. 10:16). The devil is a real being with a personality; he is sneaky and active. 1 Peter 5:7-8 says Satan roams about like a roaring lion seeking whom he may devour. Satan is serious about what he is after and ultimately wants all of humanity to bow down and worship him. Be careful because we cannot see him with our naked eyes, but he is on the prowl. But who is he after? I dare say he is after ignorant and undiscerning saints. That is saints who let their guards down, who are not alert and sober-minded.

Satan's agenda should not be news to believers. Yet many are surprised when Satan targets the saints of God to destroy us any way he can. Satan knows that we are the ones God uses to expose and frustrate his activities on the earth by the power of the Holy Spirit. We are the ones Jesus commissioned to open the eyes Satan has blinded. We are to turn them away from darkness and bring them into the light. We are to usher the deceived from the grips of the deceptive foe and lead them to Christ. God wants to receive those deceived so he can forgive them of their sins and give them an inheritance among the sanctified, by faith in Christ Jesus (Acts 26:18).

I must admit, sometimes it is unbearable to witness how Satan is deceiving the saints. Every Christian must be a born-again believer so our spiritual eyes will open; the Holy Spirit must endow us. We need to stay in constant fellowship and communion with the Holy Spirit while being sober-minded and alert to the enemy's tactics. We ought to keep our focus on the things of God, such as praying, fasting, studying the scriptures, and fellowshipping with the saints. To keep from being deceived, we must stay in constant connection. Scripture tells us that as iron sharpens iron, so a man sharpens the countenance of his friend (Prov. 27:17).

Satan knows that if he can get people to focus on the wrong things, they will eventually become passionate (worshipful) about those things. He entices until you are "hooked." He will woo your attention away from God or from seeking God, and before you know it, you are serving him. I think that is what happened to King Solomon. He began to focus on the wrong thing: he became passionate or worshipful of the wrong stuff though he started out having a passion for righteousness. Sure, he was drawn away by his own "passion," but the devil was able to entice him because of his "passion" (lust) for women.

What about you? What is that thing in your heart that attracted the devil to seek you and entice you to draw you away from worshipping God? Is it the need to be accepted? Is it guilt, shame, or the feeling of inadequacy? We often become dissatisfied with where we are in our walk with God, and we sometimes unconsciously, I suppose, attempt to find our identity or even purpose in works. It is one reason I believe we find ourselves advocating with a great passion for causes that oppose God. If we are not aligned with God's Word, Satan can subtly shift our focus and redirect our worship; Solomon is a perfect example.

Movements and Organizations

Another example is within the environmental movements or organizations. These organizations consist of people who are very passionate about saving our environment. They wish to protect the world from industrialized pollutants and prevent the natural environment's disruption for financial gain. Their desire to take care of our planet is a noble act. That was one reason God placed man in the Garden — to tend to the land and take care of it. Who does not want to breathe clean air or have beautiful places to enjoy God's creation? Everyone does. However, some people associated with these organizations are extreme in their thinking and have taken a radical approach to protect the environment. The roots of their desires are fed by spirits not associated with God.

Recently, I read a post from May Hurt Lake's Health titled "Erosion from Tahoe Fire," written by Ben Anordly. Anordly states, "Although most environmental organizations and protests are peaceful and nondestructive, a small number of environmental activists assert that radical action is sometimes necessary to defend the environment." Ben continues by stating, "A small minority of protests employ controversial tactics with the potential to harm people or property."

As indicated, some environmentalists have taken on a worshipful attitude toward "saving" the earth. Many of them do not acknowledge the Creator, who made the earth they are trying to "save." They began to worship the creation rather than the Creator. Paul talks about this behavior in the first chapter of Romans.

Sometimes these groups of people protest in a violent rage against anyone who uses nature for sustenance. For example, they vehemently object to killing animals for food and clothing. Strangely enough, some of these same objectors are the ones who petition for the right to pro-choice — women murdering their unborn babies.

I saw a bumper sticker with a picture of an animal seal and a caption that stated, "Save the Baby Humans." Quite cynical but true. People have made gods of things they are trying to "save," such as the earth and animals, while supporting death, like abortion. That is the epitome of idol worship. And we all know who or what is behind an idol. The Apostle Paul said that they sacrificed pagans made to demons (1 Cor. 10:20), and Jeremiah 16:20 said that men make their own gods.

Our inner man, or our spiritual man, was made to worship God. And therefore, the spirit of men longs to worship. But since we have inherited a sinful nature, we have been worshipping incorrectly. We take our worship meant for God and give it to dumb idol gods. Sadly, in our culture, we are seeing a vast erection of foreign gods. We have even made gods out of our ideologies.

Homosexuality, the Idol of Sexuality, the God of Pride

There is a particular idol that concerns our God, and it is the idol of homosexuality. The idol of homosexuality operates under the banner of pride. Pride is a king demon that has been seducing the saints and deceiving them into bowing down. The spirit of this idol operates through pride fueled by tolerance, discrimination, and human "rights." Pride is the spirit of Satan; he is the one who first walked in this sin. This spirit of Satan, pride, is the spirit that echoed, "BOW DOWN AND WORSHIP ME."

When you observe the behavior of most homosexuals, you will no doubt come face-to-face with this spirit. The serpent has slithered its way into almost every facet of our society and culture, crying out for tolerance and rights and echoing lies about discrimination. Because many in the church have not caved to its demand, Satan has sought new opportunities to solicit worship indirectly. You will learn one of the ways later in the book.

Satan has indirectly solicited worship through the idol of homosexuality. However, with discerning ears, many have heard the tantalizing antics of this homosexual god. "Bow down and worship me." Satan's demands have echoed throughout this nation with such force that they ring spiritually and outwardly throughout the world. These demands are forceful, violent, abusive, aggressive, vulgar, lewd, and deceptive, and they hate God. Make no mistakes; this idol aims to take territories.

Did I fail to mention this idol or god has a few offspring? Yes, lesbianism, bisexuality, transsexualism, transgenderism, queerness, and the like. This spirit is aligned with Satan's deceptive works and the antichrist, attempting to force the church of Christ to bow down to it. This homosexual god seeks its own lustful desires. It has an insatiable appetite. It beckons individuals, people groups, and countries to focus on it, feed it, and worship it.

Pride is a king demon. Remember, pride was the same spirit operating in King Nebuchadnezzar, king of Babylon, who conquered all the territories and brought them under his rule (the same way homosexuality is attempting to get the whole world under its control). Pride influenced King Nebuchadnezzar to build a nine-foot image of himself, forcing his leaders and all his province to bow down and worship it, or else. Pride stood against the Most High God to usurp His authority. And pride, the same spirit found in the LGBTQ movement, is on the move. It is moving forward at a pace like never before.

It makes me wonder what is behind the acceleration and why? I sure do not have the answer, but I would like to find out. I wonder if it has anything to do with the antichrist? Regardless, in an era that severely focuses on sexuality, just as King Nebuchadnezzar idolized himself and built his idol, Satan, too, has erected the idol of homosexuality amid our cultures. Sadly, many are flocking to it with awe and worship. If you do not believe, take a closer look at what is happening. I am sure you can see it too. There is a transformation of manhood and womanhood that is happening right before our eyes, and people accept it.

Satan's Overt Attacks

Everyone, especially most of the saints, is not on board with worshipping this idol demon. Therefore, pride is on a mission to infiltrate every church, demanding these churches and their members to bow to it for the sake of tolerance and human rights. To force the church to comply, pride launches an all-out overt attack using government and laws. Here is an example. An article that my husband sent me exemplifies Satan's mission of infiltration.

According to an article found on PJmedia.com (Tyler O'Neil, Sept. 30, 3020), the State of Virginia has passed Senate Bill 686, anti-discrimination protection for the LGBTQ people. SB 686 Bill is forcing Christian Ministries to Adopt Government Ideology or Pay $100K. According to the article, "Three Christian schools and a Christian network of pregnancy centers are suing attorney general Mark

Herring to prevent Virginia from implementing two pro-LGBTQ laws that force people of faith to adopt a particular governmental ideology under threat of punishment. The two laws purport to prevent discrimination against LGBTQ people. In reality, the laws are forcing Christian ministries to choose between violating their sincerely held religious beliefs or paying hefty fines as much as $100,000 per offense."

Pride (Satan) has solicited the governmental political systems to legitimize its agenda using the ideology of tolerance and discrimination; this is a blatant satanic attack on the church to destroy it. I would not classify this as a covert attack but rather a heinous, overt attack in the church. The paw prints of the lion are craftily embedded in this law.

This Values Act SB 686 was recently signed on a Sabbath, a day before Easter Sunday, amid the 2020 pandemic, by governor Ralph Northam. It gets even more bizarre—as if $100,000 was not enough. They want ministries or churches to hire people with different views on homosexuality and the like, who can tend to the needs of homosexuals and require them to offer health benefits that pay for gender alignment surgery. However, Christian schools and Christian pregnancy centers are fighting back.

Yet, as believers recognize the motives, travail, and take a stand, here comes another blow. It is sad when "men of God," especially in high-profile positions, are bowing down to the idol of homosexuality. Recently, Pope Francis practically gave a stamp of approval on gay civil union, shocking many Catholics (Washington Post.com, by Ryan P. Burge, Oct. 23, 2020). Why would the Pope, who supposedly represents God, commit such an act? Perhaps the spirit forcing the homosexual agenda is the same spirit working in Pope Francis? Could there be a more extensive agenda, one that includes homosexuality on a global scale? It seems so. The spirit of homosexuality is working aggressively to force the world to bow down and surrender.

Spewing Volcanos

It is no surprise. Satan has been flexing his control in and through the LGBTQ PRIDE movement for a long time. He has been lying low like an active volcano bubbling underneath the earth, waiting for an opportunity to erupt. Although there were wisps of visible smoke, many people did not see what was coming.

Sadly, many have been dumbed down with the notion and mindset of "as long as they do not bother me" or "what they do in private is their own business." Many have resorted to justifying tolerance by stating, "As long as they keep it to themselves." I say enough! How much longer will we turn a blind eye to lewdness? How much longer will we tolerate the things that are displeasing to God? How much longer will we justify ungodliness? Children of God, we must stand up and become bold for the Lord.

If we, as a people, continue to keep that stance and mindset, we will miss the enemy's overall goal. We must understand that Satan's intentions are not keeping it private or confined within bedrooms or out of the public arena. In fact, the objective is the total opposite. Satan's goal was to make the LGBTQ's mission everyone's mission. The root intention was to place LGBTQ pride on display, declare their rights, and force everyone to comply and bow down.

And if they disrupt the land and trouble the nations while achieving their mission, then so be it. Why would it concern them when their root goal is to proudly display their inherent disdain to be who God created them to be? You see, it was never stated that they wanted to keep their lifestyle within their "bedroom;" we simply assumed their motives. Satan wants us to see his real goal and desire to reject God's will with the hopes that we will bow down to his rebellion.

In the 1990s, the Holy Spirit showed me Satan's will to raise homosexuality to erode the nuclear family. Afterward, a few women and I met for prayer. I recall pleading with them about praying for what the Lord showed me. In my spirit, I could see an urgency to pray for the family, and unfortunately, these women did not receive the same revelation.

Now, we are experiencing full-blown manifestations of this spirit. I wonder if our prayers would have changed the outcome of the Marriage Equality Act. I wonder what would be the fervency of God's children if the saints suspected this underlining move? What would happen if God's children fine-tuned their ears to the spiritual realm? I am ready to find out. I am sure change will come when God's children wake up, pray, and become vigilant.

Another thing that the Holy Spirit showed me in the 1990s was the cunning way Satan is trying to infiltrate the school system to indoctrinate children. The number one goal of indoctrinating children is to create normalcy around the premise of gender neutrality. Surely both revelations have been on point. Satan has been working undercover in our government for many years to fulfill his mission.

Yes, Satan has worked on the hearts of men within the governmental political system, but he also has received support from many operations, as mentioned earlier. Many groups, aware and unaware, influenced Satan's agenda until the antichrist spirit accomplished the Marriage Equality Act that passed in 2009. Here we stand; we have witnessed the passing of a horrific act that has knocked the door wide open to same-sex marriages, all encouraged by former president BO and the Supreme Court. Unsurprisingly, this act's passing was followed with loud applause from the dark kingdom while being heard and seen from the White House. What a celebration of mockery, gallantly lighted in rainbow colors in commemoration of mocking God. Well, the church is awake now. A little too late, maybe?

The promotion of this prideful spirit took off exponentially. Eventually, we saw almost every TV network promoting the homosexual agenda as never before. They ultimately bowed down to this idol of homosexuality because Hollywood bowed down to it for years; it was permissible and acceptable behavior. It was to force us to accept a lifestyle that is contrary to God's design as standard. As I said before, many have now discovered that homosexuals never intended to keep their lifestyle private, and truthfully, they never said they wanted privacy. We assumed they wanted to keep their lifestyle private, but it turns out many want to express their desires to the entire world.

So, a subtle active volcano with only wisps of smoke erupted into a full-grown volcano spewing strange red-hot lava that flowed into every crevice of our society and culture. The banners that were half-mast are now hoisted above the statue. Yet, I found joy in spite of the current circumstance. The day the Marriage Equality Act was passed, I recall the Spirit of the Lord speaking to me, saying, "They may change the law of the land, but they can NEVER change the law of God—THE WORD OF GOD." How marvelous are His promises? Instantly, I wrote those words down. I Praise God, knowing He is always in control.

5

Satan and His Devious Ways

Devastatingly enough, the plan of Satan's prideful spirit is geared toward the vulnerable ones in our societies, the children. I believe one aspect of the homosexuality agenda is to infiltrate the educational system to indoctrinate children. The idea is to present homosexuality as a normal lifestyle. The result of the mass agenda will undoubtedly confuse children. However, over time, homosexuality will be viewed as normal, especially with some of the teachers and parents who the LGBTQ community and media have brainwashed. The devil's goal is to create confusion concerning one's identity, which will lead many into his kingdom of darkness and ultimately be destroyed by the hands of the enemy.

Do Not Bow Down

The devil's underlying mission will annihilate the family unit and ultimately destroy the nations, morally and spiritually speaking. The goal is to destroy the nations from the root, which is the family. Homosexual relationships cannot produce offspring. What will happen to a society that cannot procreate children? How will we continue our mandate of being fruitful and multiplying? Keep in mind; there will be no divine or God-ordained inception if the spirit of homosexuality continues to infiltrate our system.

Why would Satan use this idol as a means to deceive and obtain worship while destroying societies? Why hide its presence behind the spirit of homosexuality? Well, I believe the devil used this tactic because he knows that decreeing a statue bearing his lewdness in our nation would have been too obvious and would not work. Like King Nebuchadnezzar and his decree of worshipping his erected idol, the devil raised a vast homosexual idol, not of wood, stone, brass, iron nor silver and gold, but of *spirit*. You cannot see nor touch the spirit. However, the spirit is there bearing his name, *pride*.

Here it stands with rainbow-colored banners waving in its mock covenant with those who worship it. The covenant with them is for total freedom; freedom from God, freedom from religion, freedom to be who they want to be, do what they want to do, and "love" whom they choose to "love" without repercussion.

It is very interesting and not coincidental that the word pride is the slogan for the gay parade that is hosted yearly. Pride was the very sin that got Lucifer cast out of heaven; he is the originator of this same sin. One can often easily recognize this spirit by its manifestations in the homosexual person or the LGBTQ community.

Yet, as I said, the devil has planted this gigantic idol in our midst and has challenged believers to bow down or else suffer the consequences. Later I will talk about the challenges some believers encounter due to their refusal to bow down to this spirit.

However, make no mistake, the rebellious prince of darkness has found ways to solicit worship by establishing the idol of homosexuality in our government, learning institutions, health care, and entertainment, including the media. Tolerance is proclaimed as an attempt to silence God's children who oppose its agenda. Indeed, all are strategies to get the saints to surrender in adoration.

Earlier I mentioned how Satan extracts worship from anything. He and his emissaries work undercover to be undetected. Surely he would not put a lewd image of himself clothed in a rainbow banner amid our nation and force us to pay homage, of course not; that would be too obvious. Not too many would fall prey to that overt tactic.

What if he could hide his identity in movements? Movements that represent homosexuality while calling it civil rights, such as the LGBTQ community. Or perhaps he can hide in the newly arrived Black Lives Matter (BLM). And let us not forget Antifa and the Civil Rights Movement and other platforms out there.

Satan has hidden in these movements to be worshipped and to carry out his mission of destroying lives by eroding the family structure, creating identity crises, emasculating men, destroying the church, and defaming God, all while being hailed as the "god of love" the "god of justice." He will continue to hide his identity and his affiliation to these movements until he is exposed.

The devil's tactic has worked in many respects. He has convinced the highest court of the land to legalize same-sex marriage in all fifty states. Same-sex marriage has granted him the respect and honor he has pursued since his fall. We must admit he has made progress. Because this strategy works, Satan will continue to hide his identity while using deceptive means to obtain worship. If he is not exposed, he will gain more followers and more sympathizers. Sadly, Christians like Pope Francis are included in the potential followers.

Unfortunately, due to ignorance, some Christians will indirectly or directly advocate for his satanic agenda. Face it, who would have thought that this nation would see the likes of two men or two women marrying each other?

June of 2015 marked an abominable shaking in the spiritual realm. That year, during the reign of our 44th president, our Supreme Court passed the same-sex marriage law or Marriage Equality Act. Now, it may not have been an obvious abomination, but think about it. If someone built a nine-foot icon of two gay persons and told everyone to bow down or pay homage, would the members of the court concede to the act? Of course not. Perhaps most of them would have known it was wrong. Some may have recognized that the devil was the orchestrator.

When Satan influenced the highest court in the nation to pass a law legalizing same-sex marriage and called it the Marriage Act, it was indeed an act of worship. The courts bowed and led the states into *bending the knee*. They have yielded to this idol; now, every state recognizes this union as a legitimate right for all homosexuals. Satan, through his surrogates, was persistent through the years and managed to secure "marriage equality" for gays. Now everyone is forced to adhere to this law.

So you see, this sinister character has and will continue to use courts, movements, governmental systems (as he did with the 44th president of the United States), causes, and organizations to further his agenda. And I dare say he is not through. He is using the homosexual agenda to force the world to bow down to him.

Look, Satan even managed to secure a day when he openly mocks God in what is called Gay Pride Day, a day where all homosexuals, transgenders, bisexuals, queers, and the like come out to a parade, displaying how proud they are of their lifestyle. This movement started in 1970 and has gained traction throughout the years.

While we may love and sympathize with those who sincerely believe they were born this way and this is who they are, we must not lose sight that they are victims of the enemy's plan. He wants to destroy them and take them to hell. He is after their souls. Unfortunately, many of them cannot see this and label Christians or anyone who tries to minister to them as bigots, haters, and whatever name they choose to call us. Some have even gone as far as to assault those who minister openly on the streets.

Let me say this: I do not want you, the reader, thinking that I am exalting the devil in any way, nor do I want you to get the impression that I am writing it off as "the devil made me do it." Although the devil is real and he is sinister, he does not do anything without being invited in one way or the other. Human beings have wills, and God gave us the choice of choosing right or wrong, truth or lies. Unfortunately, when we provide the devil access to our life, it becomes his playing field.

Also, I am not saying that the devil is a match for God because he is not. I am merely pointing out that he is a powerful enemy, and we must be very vigilant. He is a liar and a deceiver. Therefore, scripture warns us that Satan is the adversary of God and man. He is not to be taken lightly. He destroys lives, murders, steals, and blinds eyes. The whole world is in chaos because of him. However, though he is a powerful enemy, he has been defeated by Jesus. His final destination is in the lake of fire.

In the meantime, scripture tells us to put on the full armor of God so we can stand against the wiles of the devil. Wiles are crafty tricks. We are to put on the armor of God to withstand Satan's flaming darts. Not only does the devil use lies and do crafty things, but he also throws weapons. Many of you reading this book may have already experienced some of his fiery darts, so I will not defend my arguments because scripture confirms what I am saying.

If we are not careful, as Christians, we will find ourselves compromising and bowing down to this sinister character without realizing it. So in all respect, this is a book to raise our antennas. We must be aware of the ways the devil deceives us into bowing down to him. Many of you reading this book are aware of the deception. However, many people need this education, and some require a reminder. Not to mention, some will become encouraged, as they may have similar thoughts and were afraid to express them. Whatever the case may be, we are in this together.

Althea Lemme

The Blood of Christ, the Testimony of Man

As believers, we are facing fierce opposition. Our opposition is a spiritual war, and we are all in it. The devil wants to silence us to prevent us from speaking and preaching the truth. He is afraid if just one homosexual hears and receives the truth, then that person will return to Christ. Salvation is a fearful thing for the devil. Not only will he lose captives, but the Holy Spirit will expose Satan's lies concerning homosexuality and transgenderism. He knows that a person's testimony will reach other captives and set them free. Saints of God, Satan cannot afford to let that happen. Scripture clearly states that the blood of Jesus and the believer's testimony allows us to overcome Satan. Therefore, no matter how bleak and impossible the situation may look, we must continue to testify Jesus and His power of deliverance.

I love Luke 10:18; seventy disciples went out testifying Jesus Christ and returned excited because demons were subjected to them because of the name of Jesus. Jesus replied, "I saw Satan fall like lightning from heaven." When we minister and lead one to repentance, Satan loses his balance. He is rebuked and no longer able to rail accusations against that person. Therefore, he works hard to block anyone from hearing the Gospel of Jesus Christ.

Here is an example: Recently, I was watching social media street preachers preaching the Gospel at a gay pride parade. These preachers were young guys who were so compassionate and gentle. As one young man preached the Gospel with such love, a young boy dressed as a girl came up to him and engaged him in a conversation.

Do Not Bow Down

The young boy was between the ages of twelve and fourteen. You could see he was searching. He was asking questions.

Suddenly a man with a rainbow banner barged between the young man and this preacher and began telling the young boy not to listen to the preacher. The man holding the banner convinced the young boy to leave; he practically escorted him away from the young minister. The homosexual man was vulgar to the young minister, yet the young man was very gracious and kept his composure. Those possessed with this homosexual spirit are very intolerant. Though they preach and advocate for tolerance, they preach a tolerance that agrees with their sin. Yet, they become disdained (intolerant) when their sin is addressed.

We must not let the enemy and his bullies bully us into giving up. We must not bow down. We ought to stand for truth no matter what. We are to stand and proclaim the Gospel of Jesus Christ. We must remember that Jesus came to set the captives free, and we are to do the same no matter the consequences. Do not bow down to the idol of homosexuality or its offspring transgenderism, transsexualism, etc. Instead, stand! We must not be intimidated into falling to our knees before this idol.

6

We Must Stand

What are the saints to do? Should we bow down out of fear and self-preservation? Should we bow down for the sake of tolerance, or should we stand in the face of persecution and declare the truth? I say we should stand! We stand for Jesus, we stand for truth, we stand for righteousness, and we stand for love. We stand for the love of Christ, the love of people, and those who are struggling with their identity. We stand, and we Do Not Bow Down!

Now is not the time to hide or turn back. Jesus said anyone who puts their hand to the plow and turns back is not fit for the Kingdom (Luke 9:62). The good news is, we are not standing alone. We have the Holy Spirit of God, our Helper sent by the Father in the name of Jesus, to gird us with strength and wisdom. Without Him, we are no match for the evil one.

We also have our brothers and sisters in Christ. Our siblings in the Lord have laid down their lives to stand for the Gospel of Christ despite the enemy's attacks. Specifically speaking, the apostles who are like Paul, Peter, Stephen, and many others in the Bible. They have made up their mind to stand just like Daniel and the three Hebrew boys Shadrach, Meshach, and Abednego, who were among the captives in Babylon. We are very familiar with their story. Daniel and the three Hebrew boys stood against the pompous King Nebuchadnezzar, king of Babylon, who ordered them to bow down and worship his golden statue. These young men refused to comply despite the danger of being thrown into a fiery furnace. Despite the threats on their lives, these Hebrew boys decided they would rather suffer death than deny the Lord, their God.

Daniel also had his challenges. After Nebuchadnezzar's reign and under Darius of Persia's rule, Daniel, being chosen by Darius for a promotion, was set up by enemies. The trap was to get Daniel to stop praying to his God and pray to King Darius for thirty days. Do you notice the familiar scenario? Most often, there are snares in place to cause us to abandon our devotion to God. Although there was a thirty-day decree for all to worship king Darius, the masked agenda was to woo Daniel away from God and get him to bow down to Darius. Daniel was resilient and only prayed to his God, God Almighty.

Daniel never ceased praying, and there are three reasons why he prayed continuously. First, Daniel was a Jew; second, Jews were commanded not to worship any god but the God of heaven and earth;

and third, Daniel was a man of prayer who prayed three times a day. Therefore, his refusal to comply with this new law of not praying to his God earned him a death sentence.

Daniel was proclaimed guilty, and he was to be thrown into the lions' den. When King Darius sentenced Daniel to the lions' den, the lions were supposed to devour him, but the Lord shut the lions' mouths, and Daniel lived. Because of God's supernatural intervention, neither Daniel nor the three boys were harmed. Daniel and the three Hebrew boys were determined not to bow down to man or idols, even if God did not rescue them.

Modern Day Lions' Den

Here in the West, saints are not sentenced to a lion's den nor burning furnaces, at least not yet. However, we are faced with movements, media, and laws that attempt to silence our voices and force us to bow down to things that are in direct conflict with God's righteousness. In addition, we have homosexuality, transgenderism, same-sex marriages, abortions, racism, radical feminism, and immoral and lewd conduct. Not to mention, there are also anti-government conducts, anti-Christian movements, and other organized groups such as Black Lives Matter, Antifa, Planned Parenthood, and the LGBTQ community. All these movements, and many more, are controlled by surrogates for Satan and his demons.

At times, it may feel like we are in the lions' den or the fiery furnace, especially when we speak against antichrist movements. Satan uses these means to force us to bow down. One of his most infamous things to use against the saints is the law. When a decree was issued for Daniel and all the provinces to bow down, it was no coincidence. It was a strategy of the enemy. Be aware; Satan continues to use the same approach against the saints. That is why he and his demons are so heavily involved in social justice movements. They are accessible pathways to execute his mission.

These movements and their supporters are under Satan's influence and have railed against the saints of God. For example, I watched a video of a black pastor who got assaulted by the BLM "protestors." These protesters chanted, "F* your Jesus!" They ostracize the saints for defending our rights to give voice to our faith and beliefs while they hypocritically promote fairness, equality, and free speech. They condemn the saints for doing the very things they claim they are advocating for themselves. These organizations and their members and supporters attack believers, calling them bigots, intolerant, haters, homophobic, and Islamophobic.

There are also attacks against what some deemed as "white evangelical Christians." There may be the sin of partiality within the churches, but there is no such thing as black evangelicals or white evangelicals. It is a tactic of the devil to keep the Body of Christ divided through hate. We are all a part of one Body, and that is the Body of Christ. I do not doubt that the sin of partiality is in the Body of Christ. We must address partiality, or we will find ourselves among the herd of goats when our Lord returns.

Nonetheless, Satan influences many movements, and in turn, they are influential in our culture. These movements are very vulnerable to him, to the point that he can use them to carry out his bidding while leading them to their demise.

Please hear what I am saying: Satan does not do anything new! It is the same old tricks, placed in new bags! Satan has been a liar and a thief from the beginning. He has connections in high places that carry out his plans, whether overtly or covertly. He has connections with political leaders and members of the secular communities, media, entertainment, etc. But we must stand. Despite Satan's ties, our fellowship with the Father surpasses all relationships the devil has.

We Must Stand

We have connections with our El Elyon, the Most High God. Our relationship is with the King of kings, God of all gods, Lord of lords, and Prince of Peace. We have the backings of heaven. If you have doubts or fear, Daniel 9:21, 23, and 10:13-14; 2 Kings 6:15; 2 Chronicles 20:15-17; and Acts 12:5-17 and 16:23-26 are excellent reads.

Although it may appear as if there are more of them than there are of us, do not let the roar of the toothless lion scare you. Many believers are frozen with fear. Fear of retaliation, fear of losing businesses, fear of losing livelihood, or fear of losing reputation. How important are those things compared to the things God has prepared for those who love Him? Our eyes have not seen, neither our ears heard, neither has it entered into men's hearts of the things that God has prepared for those who genuinely love Him (1 Cor. 2:9). If we love Him, we must speak and speak with boldness.

We must preach the love of God and His Kingdom. We must preach against evil and unrighteousness and no longer keep silent. As a naturalizing citizen of the United States, I have learned that in times past, believers have kept quiet on issues they should have stood up against. Many believe the church should only preach to men's souls and not get involved in controversial or political issues. Gratefully, we have now realized that was a mistake. Thus, some believers who are finally taking a stand are the ones who realized their mistake of remaining silent.

Even now, those who decided they were not getting involved with politics are learning from our history. In the past, evidence has shown that churches that have taken a passive are not effective. Passivity should no longer be our stance. I believe this is one of the reasons we are fighting so hard. Yet, believe it or not, some believers still hold to the views that we should not get involved, even today. It is unfortunate.

Politics or No Politics?

Should the church stay out of politics seeing that everything has become political in our nation? Should we keep silent for the sake of not becoming too political? Better yet, should we cower like a petrified child in a corner who is scared of an ant? No! I think not!

The early church did not stop preaching the Gospel even in the face of persecution. Paul preached while in chains and executed. Peter stood and preached amid persecution and was eventually crucified (upside down). Stephen was stoned, James was killed, John the Revelator was banished to an island called Patmos.

And while it is not necessarily the early church as in the New Testament, who could forget David? The young man, David, stood against a mocking giant three times his height. David did not cower at the sight of the "uncircumcised Philistine," as he referred to Goliath. He took that giant down with a slingshot (1 Sam. 17:26).

Jesus is our Commander and Chief; He is our Sling Shot. The Holy Spirit is the Rock in our sling. Christians who are followers of Jesus Christ, sons of God, must STAND and wage war against Satan to avoid falling under his influence.

God gave us spiritual weapons to wage war. Worldly weapons will not topple this giant; our weapons are only mighty through God. Scripture tells us that "the weapons of our warfare are not carnal—not flesh and blood, not human power—but mighty through God to the pulling down of strongholds" (2 Cor. 10:4). God has instructed us to put on the whole armor of God. We must clothe ourselves in the helmet of salvation, the breastplate of righteousness, shield of faith, belt of truth, and sandal of peace, and lastly, we must take up the sword of the Spirit, which is the word of God—the written word of God. Yet, having done what God commanded us, we must **stand!**

Consecrate yourself

We must spend time in prayer, so we can hear and receive direction from God. Prayer keeps us nonelected to heaven; prayer keeps us connected to heaven. David was connected to heaven because he worshipped and prayed a lot. Because of his communion with God, David was endued with the Holy Spirit and defeated Goliath with a slingshot and a small smooth stone. Through prayer, we too have the power to uproot, tear down, build up, and cast out (Jeremiah 1:10).

Do Not Bow Down

We should not grow weary. However, if we do, we must remember that God is our refuge and strength, and God is a very present help in times of trouble. Therefore, though the mount quake and shake at its foaming, we will not be moved (Psalms 46:3).

It may not seem like it, but we are fighting a winning battle. We have already won the war. Jesus defeated Satan and regained possession of the kingdom (earthly), and gave it back to whoever will come to Him. Be of great cheer, the people who know their God will do exploits (Daniel 11:32). We, the followers of Christ, know our God, and because we know our God, we know who we are. We are victorious over every satanic power and principality standing against us on the earth.

Know this truth; Satan is on the earth illegally. He is no longer the god of this world. Jesus said in John 12:31, while speaking of his impending death, "now is the god of this world cast out." When Jesus died on the cross, He took dominion of the earth and returned it to the children of God. So then, the enemy no longer has authority or power over men or this world.

Satan's ability to control and influence is due to a lack of knowledge. Those who are informed are engaged in a war against him. Though Jesus has dismantled Satan's power at the cross, he is still fighting to retain it. One of the reasons I believe we are engaged in spiritual warfare.

Satan wants to hold on to power, and he is using the innocent, the wicked, the ignorant, and the unsuspecting people to do his work. Child of God, do not be a part of those innocent, susceptible people that the devil uses. However, many will suffer discomfort; I will not deny it. We are In a war; we will experience some blows, incur losses, and even suffer some casualties, but we must stand and fight! God is with us! Jesus Christ is our Rock. He has already won the victory for us. Fear not! **DO NOT BOW DOWN!**

7

No Compromise

Laws and Commands

Most believers like myself are pretty compassionate people. We do not like to see injustice done to others. We despise the intentional sufferings of others, especially those who are weak and disadvantaged. We understand that sometimes people are dealt a hard hand in life. Face it, life comes with trials and pain, and sometimes at no fault of the individuals; we get that.

We also believe that people have the freedom to express themselves the way they choose. It is one of the reasons God gave us free will; so that we can make choices. However, God's earnest desire is for us to make the right choices, not the wrong ones. For example, in Deuteronomy 30:19, God said, behold, I set before you this day life and death; choose life. Often, the belief is that it is ok to make the wrong choice; however, it is not God's will for us to make choices that are outside of His divine purpose and plans for us.

Nevertheless, people make choices and many wrong ones. They make bad choices in what they do and in what they say. We may not like what is said, but we must respect others' views, even if those views go against both our views and God's views.

Freedom of speech and freedom of expression are provisions made in the U.S constitution to assure our God-given rights are protected. However, while we have the freedom to speak and express ourselves, our society has laws and standards by which we are governed. These laws are to protect individuals as well as our society at large. Face it, if we did not have laws nor standards, then lawlessness and lewdness would run rampant.

The same is true for the Kingdom of God. God has laws of righteousness for His children to adhere. We may sympathize with people who have been hurt and those who are hurting, being treated unfairly or unjustly. Still, if they violate the laws of God, which are the highest standard for men, then we cannot be sympathetic to evil or that which goes against God's laws and standards. Jeremiah 11:14-15 is a perfect reference for this statement.

Sin is a violation of God's standards, and anyone who sins goes against God; that person is a sinner no matter who that person is or what that person feels—bottom line. Scripture tells us that there is no one good, no not one, **all**, even those who have experienced hardship and pain, **all** have sinned and have fallen short of the glory of God (Romans 3:23). All means you and me, but the Blood of Jesus redeems us.

Do Not Compromise

Romans 5:12 said we were once worthy of God's judgment; therefore, we must not condemn anyone, and we must not condone their sins. And here is the big one, *we must not compromise with evil and with those who sin.* We must love those who are sinning, but we must not condone their sins. Recall the man who the apostle Paul wrote off, having an affair with his stepmother, and Paul instructed those elders to put him from amongst them until he repented? That was a no tolerance, no compromise move they were to take. It did not matter the circumstances; it did not matter how much they liked each other or whether they were two consenting adults. They violated God's holy Word. Unless repentance occurred, they would experience God's judgment.

Was Paul unloving? Was he a bigot? The answer to both questions is no. Was he intolerant? Yes, he was intolerant to sin and would not permit it to destroy the church. Jesus, the Master, and the One who called him to ministry did not condone sin. Instead, Jesus called sinners to repentance. Therefore, we must follow Jesus' example. We should have the confidence in God to stand on what He declares righteous.

However, the questions remain. Do we have confidence in our God, like Jesus Christ did when He walked the earth? Are we as confident as Paul and the Apostles? Are we confident in our identity in Jesus Christ? Is Christ our all-sufficient God? Sad to say, but many of us are not as confident as we should be.

Many of my fellow believers in Christ have compromised with those who railed against God's righteous standards. They have succumbed to compromising because of fear of being labeled or rejected. Therefore, they have settled with accepting lewdness and turning a blind eye to sin.

For example, Chick-Fil-A came under attack because of their stand on speaking against same-sex marriage. At the time, I thought it was a bold stance. This fast-food restaurant is also known to be a Christian entity. They had standards, so I thought. One of their criteria was to remain closed on Sundays to honor God. Because of their policy, it has allowed employees to go to their prospective place of worship — if they choose.

I believe almost every Christian applauded Chick-Fil-A for honoring the Lord's Day. However, years later, battling with this giant idol of Homosexuality and same-sex marriages. Chick-Fil-A was protested against by the LGBTQ community and its affiliates. Because the company's president exercised freedom of speech, he came under scrutiny for disagreeing with same-sex unions.

The fast-food chain endured the persecution. Chick-Fil-A endured boycotts by many of the LGBTQ communities, and yet, they did not bow down nor compromise. They also took a stand after coming under fire for their support of Godly faith-based organizations.

Unfortunately, my heart sunk when I learned that Chick-Fil-A compromised. They bowed down under the pressure of the LGBTQ community and its supporters. They have decided not to support Christian-based organizations like the Salvation Army, Christian athletics organizations, or organizations that do not support the LGBTQ community.

The example with Chick-Fil-A illuminates that Satan would do anything to get the saints of God to bow down to him, or he will attempt to destroy us. He adds pressure until he achieves his goal. Only those whose branches are attached to the true Vine will stand and not back down. However, what I found to be disheartening is that a coffee café, 'the coffee giant,' has the freedom to displays LGBTQ emblem showing their support openly. At the same time, "Christian" businesses are bullied until they cower into a corner.

My question is, what or whose values or standards were Chick-Fil-A standing on? What was their purpose of standing up and then bowing down? The Hebrew boys and Daniel did not bend the knee; despite the fact they were facing death, they did not compromise. Unfortunately for Chick-Fil-A, the adversary brought them to their knees, very sad indeed.

We must not compromise, even if it means a financial loss. We serve a God who is mighty. Surely God will grant us favor; even if He does not, we should not bow down nor compromise with the evil of this world. We should take the words of Esther, "if I perish, I perish," or we should be like David and demand, "who is this uncircumcised Philistine, who dares mock our God?"

Principalities in High Places

Despite the media's portrayal, the LGBTQ community is a small minority group of people—percentage-wise. Yet, this popular fast-food chain that seemed to uphold Christian values buckled under them. The LGBTQ has significantly impacted our culture and society and had a tremendous impact on Christian businesses. The LGBTQ's influence is so grand that they managed to rewrite the laws to match their benefit.

They have laws enacted that protect their "rights" and seek to indoctrinate the masses with their ideas on human sexuality and gender identity. They have influenced every system and industry in our society, i.e., the educational system, political system, the entertainment industry, and the like. The LGBTQ's purposes have manifested because of the powerful spiritual influence working behind them. The influence is beyond the natural realm; it is supernatural.

Some people do not see the supernatural powers of darkness with this minority group of people; however, they are there. Unfortunately, unless one is born-again and walking in the Spirit, you may not recognize that the influence behind them is none other than the chief of pride; Satan. I pray that this group wake up and not take for granted the reality of the Holy Spirit and our supernatural God. I pray they understand that Satan and his demons are our defeated evil enemy. I also pray that they realize the reality of this darkness and how detrimental it is to their soul if they ignore it

It is equally detrimental, even downright dangerous, when believers are among the many that ignore the supernatural, demonic realms working in the children of disobedience (those in rebellion against God's standards). Sadly, many "believers" do not believe that realm exists; many believe that God is the only spiritual being. I understand, some only want to focus on God, and there is nothing wrong with that. However, scripture tells us that the spiritual realm exists and Satan and demons are real. So to acknowledge God and not the enemy is unbalanced and not biblical.

Out of fear, some believers do not believe that Satan and demons exist, or they believe in their existence but do not care to address it. I will say this: those who fear the devil do not know God and therefore have no knowledge of Satan, demons, and how they influence our day-to-day choices. They have no idea what they are up against and have become victims of his deceptions in many ways.

Ephesians chapter 6 reminds us that the supernatural realm is real and Satan and demons are real beings. It reminds us that we are in a battle with them every day. Ephesians 6:12 says, "For we wrestle not against flesh and blood but against principalities, against powers, against the rulers of the darkness of this world, against spiritual wickedness in high places." So yes, we are always in contact with spiritual forces, and these forces work through people—flesh and blood. The LGBTQ community is a perfect example. The LGBTQ community consists of real beings who are gravely influenced by the demonic spiritual realm.

Reasons LGBTQ Influence our Community and Culture

It is no surprise; the LGBTQ community has infiltrated our nations in more ways than we can count. Therefore, we will simply cover six reasons and causes for the influence that LGBTQ has today.

1. *They receive support and backing from the demonic spiritual realm.*

As much as we would like to hold people responsible for their actions, and they should be held accountable, we cannot dismiss the truth that the LGBTQ community is under control and is being used by Satan.

2. *They have fierce determination and drive to be accepted.*

Homosexuals experienced rejection in some manner. The need to be approved stems from the truth that they have suffered some sort of rejection. Therefore, they perceive the Gospel of Christ as God and His messengers rejecting them. As a result, all who preach the Good News are considered unloving, hateful, or preaching "hate speech" and discrimination.

3. *They are persistent in the fight for recognition and acceptance.*

The LGBTQ community finds their identity in their sexuality. Therefore they must fight to be accepted and approved, or they will never feel whole until their desires are satisfied. Also, to be accepted or approved, release their conscience from sin.

4. *They have support from sympathizers who are liberal in their thinking.*

Many benefit from the homosexual agenda and will do anything to promote their cause. Additionally, some are genuine about the homosexual plight and want to help them. These individuals believe that people can choose to "love" whom they want to "love." As a result, they influence legislation, marches, and the various systems that govern our nation.

    5. <u>The attitude of the saints has become dismissive.</u>

Many believers have taken a 'blind-eye approach by stating, "as long as they keep it in their bedroom." Then, some choose to preach repentance and the Gospel of Jesus Christ to the saved. Many neglected their role and responsibility of reaching the loss by focusing on 'themselves' and the 'Church.' This stance is unacceptable within the Kingdom of Heaven, yet, some Christians are passive and lazy and do not want to engage in spiritual warfare nor reach the lost.

    6. <u>The unloving responses toward the homosexual.</u>

Homosexuals have had enough rejection, and being ministered to without the love of Christ can cause even greater damage to their souls. The Gospel must be clothed in love. Indeed, the Gospel is the expression of God's love to ALL sinners.

<u>The Love of God Compels</u>

In reason six, I state 'responses' because there is a difference between responding with love and truth and being outright mean and nasty. We are to speak the truth in love. As I eluded earlier, many of the LGBTQ's are crying out for love and acceptance. So we must always be led by the Holy Spirit and minister in a way that brings repentance, not condemnation.

I have seen testimonies of homosexuals rejected by the church or believers and resulted in a disdain for the Church and God. I have also seen the church embrace, love, and not compromise the truth of the Gospel; thus, those individuals received salvation. Jesus' encounter and conversation with the Women at the Well in John 4 is a perfect example of winning over a sinner.

Jesus is our Wonderful Counselor, Mighty God, Everlasting Father, and Prince of Peace. They need everything that Jesus is and everything that Jesus has. Therefore, we must do all we can to bring them to Jesus. However, we must never confuse compassion with passivity or permission to sin. We must never compromise the truth as some of our brothers and sisters are doing today.

As far as I see, many have compromised the Gospel of Christ to pacify sin. They are preaching a feel-good Gospel to those who are perishing. Many preach what I call a psychological Gospel, a Gospel that caters to the emotions rather than preaching the fullness of Christ. It is time to say **enough!**

Preach in Spirit and Truth

Many of us are like the Pharisees Jesus rebuked In Mark chapter 7. Jesus called the Pharisees hypocrites because they compromised the commandments of God for the traditions of men. They refrained from obeying the Word of God and heeded the traditions of the elders. Instead of the Pharisees following the law, they followed the elders' customs because it was convenient. They were in tune with scripture yet watered it down to be relevant. 2 Timothy 3:5 echoes even louder, "having a form of godliness but denying the power thereof" (KJV).

Also, I wonder if keeping our tax-exempt status or fear of losing it has caused us to bow to man's regulations of the Church? Maybe in the name of separation of Church and State, we feel we must abide by governmental <u>regulations concerning religious views or lose our tax-exempt status?</u>

    I believe many pastors are afraid to preach, teach, or do anything that the government will deem a violation of Church and State. As saints, we must never forget that the Church is the body of Christ. We belong to Christ. Our rights and freedom were given first by the Almighty God.

    We should not be bound by the laws of man when it comes to the preaching of the Gospel. We have a mandate from our God to preach the Gospel; to open the eyes of the blind and turn them from darkness to light. We are to preach, teach, heal the sick, and cast out devils. The Church, at least some, has not fulfilled the Great Commission, especially many U.S. ministers. We must get back to ministering in the power of Jesus to save sinners, even to those in the sin of homosexuality.

    When it comes to homosexuality, there should be no compromising of the Gospel, though some in the Body have compromised. Pastors, who claim to be a follower of Christ and the pastor of a Bible-believing Christian church, should not be officiating same-sex "marriages." In my opinion, any pastor or lay ministers who officiate same-sex marriages have placed themselves in direct opposition to God and rented their souls to the devil. They are no better than Balaam, who rented his service to Balak to perform witchcraft against God's people.

    The person or persons who ordain same-sex marriages creates a spiritual disservice to the homosexual couple by agreeing with their union and not warning them to turn from this sin against God.

Whether they listened or not, pastors, ministers, and believers must speak up and warn against same-sex marriages. God is a just God and does not take lightly to those who set their heart against Him.

Beloved, we must be careful not to compromise with the homosexual idol and its agenda as some in the body have done. Instead, we must point them to the truth whenever possible. Be aware this is a spirit that desires to bring everyone into an agreement with it. It uses a victim's mentality to gain sympathy to trap those walking according to this world's wisdom and men's traditions.

Be warned! For such a one, Satan is seeking your soul to bring you into an agreement with him. Be aware that this spirit is the same serpent that beguiled Eve into agreeing with its explanation of knowledge and death. Yes, the deceiver, the one who entered the serpent and deceived Eve. This one draws the whole world using the same tactics; Remember, he does not have new tricks. Be alert lest he beguiles you.

8

Love, Not Compromise

As saints, we are commanded to love. Jesus commands us to love our enemies and pray for them. Therefore, we must love and intercede on their behalf. We have only one enemy, and that is Satan and his evil angels. The LGBTQ community is not our enemy; they are people like you and me. We were once sinners walking in darkness, just as they are, but the grace of God has touched our lives through Jesus Christ.

We are no longer in darkness; we are in the light. Therefore, we ought not to walk in darkness but rather walk in the light. As the light of this world, we are a living reflection of Christ's love. The light we bear is the path for those who are walking in darkness. Without the option of an illuminated direction, those walking in darkness will become lost. Those in darkness need to see God's light in us. His light is His love meant for all souls (John 3:16).

However, while God called us to love homosexuals, we cannot join them to advance their ungodly agenda. Their views in life and their lifestyle of homosexuality is in direct opposition with God's plans and purpose for their lives and all humanity.

Their agenda is an arrangement set forth by Satan, who works through all who are in rebellion against God. Many of them are politicians and lawmakers working to fulfill Satan's mission. They are filled with the spirit of the antichrist and with an agenda to destroy the church. As 1 John 4:3 says, these are the antichrist seeds whose spirit is already here in this world. Considering the season that we are now in, I believe the antichrist is already here, waiting for certain events to take place where he can emerge.

As believers, we support the antichrist if we join organizations, movements, or causes that bear the antichrist's mark. When I say antichrist mark, I mean actions and attitude of anyone who stands against or opposes and denies the deity of Jesus Christ and that Jesus Christ is the Son of God who came in the flesh. The Holy Spirit is a spirit we cannot see, but we can see and experience His manifestations. We are sealed with the promised Holy Spirit. Likewise, the antichrist is a spirit, and as the Holy Spirit, it is not detectable by the natural eyes. However, you can see and experience the manifestations of the antichrist spirit in movements, organizations, people, etc.

Additionally, we have agreed with the antichrist spirit if we aid through our finances or offer any support to further their agenda.

We must be mindful of who and what we come into agreement with. We must understand that spiritually or physically, willingly or unintentionally, if we have yoked ourselves with demonic entities in any fashion, then we have come into agreement with their causes.

However, if a believer supports demonic entities and later finds out about the enemy's agenda, they must repent and renounce their participation. If a believer becomes aware of their affiliation with satanic movements, denies the Holy Spirit's unction, and continues to support these agendas, then God will judge.

Do not be afraid to stand for what is true according to God's Word. We will receive accusations. The world will claim we are not loving, not being Christians. Many will argue that we are not Christians or that Christians are hateful. However, the world's claims and accusations should not move believers to compromise. We should know that we will receive facetious claims. Therefore, we must realize that the devil is having a tantrum, and the accuser is ranting.

We must not forge relationships with the world. Remember, the scripture said, "Friendship with the world is to be enemy with God" (James 4:4). We must know where our loyalty lies. As King Jehoshaphat found out, there should be no room for compromise.

King Jehoshaphat's story serves as a sobering reminder of God's displeasure with those who align themselves with His enemies. In 1 Chronicles 2:20-37, King Jehoshaphat was the king of Judah, and King Ahaziah (son of King Ahab and Jezebel, 1 King 22-53), was the king of Israel who scripture said did wickedly. They were the same Israelites whom God delivered from their Egyptian oppressors, except the kingdom was split, the northern kingdom, which was the

Israelites, and the southern kingdom, which was Judah. King Jehoshaphat, king of Judah, did what was right in God's sight, while Ahaziah, king of Israel, followed his parents' footsteps and did evil.

King Jehoshaphat and his kingdom were set to be destroyed, but God delivered and saved him and his kingdom. Yet, King Jehoshaphat decided to join in a money-making merger with the king of Israel. However, their business did not take off because God eliminated their coalition by destroying their ships. King Jehoshaphat allied with the king of Israel, and God was not pleased. The Lord showed His displeasure by destroying the vessels they built together.

The warning in this story is not to align ourselves with those who oppose God, even if it seems like a good cause. It is imperative that we do not join forces with those who are against God, or we might find ourselves fighting with God. Yes, we are under grace, but God is not mocked: "Whatsoever a man soweth, that shall he also reap" (Gal. 6:7, KJV). Paul asked the question in 2 Corinthians 6:14: "What fellowship has righteousness with lawlessness and what communion has light with darkness?" Frankly, the whole verse tells us how the Holy Spirit feels about our association with those who disagree with God's position on sin.

I am not implying that God is going to destroy anyone. I am merely pointing out His displeasure with His people who join forces with His enemies. One must repent and renounce their association with ungodliness lest they experience its consequences. Either we will break off whatever relationship we have forged with these groups, or God will do it for us. Scripture tells us that whom God loves, He chastises.

God is furious when the Gospel is compromised because the love of God is in the Gospel of Jesus Christ. The power and love of God must be demonstrated through the preaching of the Gospel and revealed by the Holy Spirit. People bound by the spirit of Homosexuality need the Gospel of Jesus Christ; therefore, we must uphold the integrity of God's Word.

Forget the World's View of Sin. What Does God Say?

We, the saints of God, should not compromise the Gospel for humanistic and scientific thinking. We must not bow down to humanistic and scientific explanations on what God constitutes as sin. Many saints have researched life and human behaviors from these perspectives; scientific and humanistic. They have placed their stamp of approval and deemed scientific and humanistic research reliable and having the ultimate authority. Thus some have compromised the Gospel of Christ by watering down God's truth, saying, "God loves homosexuals," or that they have the right to get "married," and imply they were born gay. No one was born gay. However, demons can infect our bloodline or hold legal claims to a person from birth due to their family's involvement in dark arts, witchcraft, or any type of idolatry, including sexual perversion.

Some in the field of counseling may feel that science and psychology have proven the case for homosexuality, giving it legitimacy. I have not met a Bible-believing pastor who would agree with either, but it does not mean that there are not some who agree.

However, despite conclusions reached, the school of science and psychology must answer to the authority of scripture. 2 Timothy

3:16-17 states, "All scripture is given by inspiration of God, and is profitable for doctrine, for reproof, for correction, for instruction in righteousness." When we read Romans 15:4, it states similar sentiments: "Whatever things were written before were written for our learning." In synopsis, God gave the Bible for our instruction, knowledge, and understanding of Him and our relationship to Him (God). Therefore, the Bible reigns supreme.

Unfortunately, we have made humanistic and scientific ideas the authority above the Bible. We have exchanged the power of God for human reasoning. Since we have made these venues the rules on human behaviors, we have found ourselves compromising the word of God; such is from the pit of hell.

Satan is a liar and a deceiver, and as told by Jesus, there is no truth in him. Whatever he whispers in our ears is a lie. Do not be deceived; Satan will speak a twisted version of the truth with an intent to deceive. That is what he does, and he is excellent at it.

A Twisted Version Is a Lie

Recently, I was in a conflict with someone I know very well. At first, we were having a conversation. Then it suddenly escalated. The antichrist spirit began to manifest. It was pretty disturbing for me to see how the enemy can make people believe his lies. There was such vile hatred toward evangelical Christians' specific race that I will not mention; perhaps you can guess which group.

This person denounced evangelical Christians as racist while expressing the same racist, hateful attitude and behavior toward the group. There was no reasoning with such a mindset. It got more bizarre when the person asked me if I would attend a gay and lesbian church. The person expressed that God loves them too, as if I said something hateful toward homosexuals. This person was subscribing to the current narrative that Christians hate homosexuals or gay people. Some Christians hate homosexuals, but to assume that all Christians hate gays is just unfounded.

I have prayed and spoken into the life of someone who struggled with same-sex attraction. That person, through the help of many others, is now living a life free in Christ Jesus. The person with whom I had a conflict was very hostile toward me. It was clear that the enemy had a hold somewhere in that person's mind. I will not say the person is not a believer, though they are not grounded in their faith in Christ and are living or attempting to live out of two opposing views.

No More Double-Mindedness

The battle of living in two opposing views is called *double-mindedness*. Sadly, many Christians walk a double-minded lifestyle. These are Christians who walk in carnality (flesh), who hardly study the Word of God, and whose knowledge and wisdom derive from a humanistic perspective. These are those who have a form of godliness but deny the power of God even to reveal His truth.

They live out of their soul; they are soulish Christians. Sad to say, but this individual whom I had a conflict with is not the only one who claimed to know Jesus and is giving credence to the homosexual churches. They have recognized these churches as *normal* and are trying to convince or even bully others into paying homage to the idol of homosexuality.

Next, we have Christians who do not know who they are. They are double-minded Christians. These double-minded believers desire to be loved by the world while following Jesus. 1 John 2:15 said not to love the world or the things in it; if we do, then the love of the Father is not in us. We have to choose who we will follow. Double-minded believers will argue and defend what the Bible calls ungodly to sound intelligent and relevant.

Choose This Day Who You Will Serve

Jesus said it plainly. To understand the ways of Jesus, one must be born again. Jesus also made it clear that no man can serve two masters. Therefore, one cannot claim to follow Jesus and follow the world at the same time. One must make a choice. There are no swing votes. There is no compromising with God; it is Jesus or the world. Simple.

As believers, we cannot afford to be double-minded Christians. Being double-minded will makes us unstable in *all* our ways, whether it be in our devotion to Christ, our ability to stand for righteousness, or our commitment to our brothers and sisters of the faith.

Lastly, being double-minded is ineffective in the Kingdom of God. Being like the world or loved by the world is not our mission. We are to share the Gospel of Jesus Christ and His Kingdom with the world. We must make a decision that we will stand for God. We must stand and not compromise, even if we have to stand alone.

Althea Lemme

We are the church, the bride of Christ. Our devotion should be to our Groom, Jesus Christ. The bride of Christ must not compromise with this deviant, whoring, lying, manipulating, and destructive spirit of homosexuality — not the person, but the satanic spirit working in them, the spirit of the antichrist. We must not commit fornication with it.

Althea Lemme

9

Satan Is an Opportunist

When we were children, my siblings, cousins, and friends from our neighborhood hitched rides from tractors driven to the farm. We would lie and wait in the grass for the tractor, and as it passed, we would spring from the grass and attempt to hitch a ride on the back. We jumped at the opportunity of hitching a ride, literally. As we waited for rides, we experienced more failed attempts than successes. Though it was pretty dangerous, we always laughed at the experience because whoever drove that tractor was not a happy camper.

At times, my cousin would get lucky, and someone would give her a ride. However, nothing changed; we also attempted to hitch the rides my cousin received. Often the drivers had no idea what we were doing until they saw or heard us chasing their truck. Those were some good times; we were children, looking for an opportunity to enjoy ourselves. I suppose you could have called us opportunists since we were always scouting ways to enjoy a free ride.

Likewise, I say to you, be aware; Satan is an opportunist! He is always looking for opportunities to hitch a ride undetected. 1 Peter 5:8 said our adversary the devil is like a roaring lion seeking whom he may devour. Satan and his demons are always on the prowl looking for opportunities (situations) where he can undertake.

Satan studies our actions and attitudes, so he knows who he can agitate easily. His game is to get us to slip up, so he and his demons can dive right in. That is why in the same verse, Peter told us to be sober-minded and vigilant. As believers, we must be alert in all areas of our lives; if we are not, we may find ourselves being harassed or taken captive by Satan and his demons at will.

We must understand that if we provide the opportunities for him to take control, he will act. Coincidently, we should not be surprised if we find ourselves being manipulated and used by him. Therefore, We must not leave open doors that Satan can manipulate and walk through. Sadly, many of us have found ourselves in situations where we were used and controlled by the evil one. Even further, we have also pondered questions such as, "How did this happen?" or "How did I get here?" The answer, we were not sober-minded, much less vigilant; we were not alert to evil. I, too, am guilty of that.

Though you must know, as an opportunist—the devil or Satan (whichever name you wish to call him) will come to you at your most vulnerable moments. It could be when your attention is on other things or when you have experienced abuse, sexually, physically, mentally, verbally, or emotionally. Additionally, Satan loves to grab people by the tail, especially when they struggle with bouts of doubt about themselves or their abilities.

Most importantly, Satan loves to whisper thoughts in your ears, thoughts filled with lies. He is so subtle that you might believe Satan's thoughts are your thoughts. He lies and deceives you in so many ways to get you to believe and trust his voice. You may say, "The devil cannot fool me," or "He cannot come near me." Listen, if the devil was bold enough to sit before God submitting accusations concerning Job, why do you think he cannot come near you? He is leviathan, the lurking serpent waiting for an opportunity to lunge at its victims.

There are reasons we must put on the whole armor of God. Even further, after we have put on the full armor of God, we must do as scripture states and stand. We must be alert, sober-minded, and vigilant. The devil is not looking outside of the waters watching you; like a sea serpent, he is lurking in the murky water. So if you are wading in dark waters of ignorance, supporting those who stand against God because you feel offended, or because you have been a victim of racism, or any form of -isms, you have opened yourself to becoming a victim of leviathan.

Hear me; the devil will use wicked people to do evil things. The devil intends to entice people to carry out acts of violence and manipulate situations to stir pain, unrest, and protests. And, yes, I said evil people. Every person was born with the propensity to sin. Due to man's fall, I believe everyone has the seed of the evil one in their DNA.

However, it is essential to note that the devil does not do anything without an invitation. So claiming or blaming the devil for our evil actions gives him more credit than he deserves. However, he does tempt and lure us with what we desire. He is an opportunist, which is why Peter may have called him a roaring lion, seeking his prey.

Yet, the real question remains. Why is Satan roaming? Satan roams because he is not omnipresent. He cannot be everywhere at the same time as God. Satan also roams because he is not omniscient. He is not all-knowing as our Father. Therefore, Satan has to go back and forth, scanning the entire earth looking for his prey — as he did in Job 1.

Surrogate of Use

As of late, there have been numerous protests and rallies. While most of those expressions of speech started with good intentions, Satan has roamed within those missions. Thus something that should have resulted in a positive change and impact escalated into something dominated by the spirit of rebellion and hatred toward God.

To be specific, the Black Lives Matter Movement has been seized by Satan to advance his campaign of homosexuality. Satan cleverly used this movement to deceive God-fearing men and women into bowing down to his spell. As I reflect on the words I heard that one morning, "Bow down and worship me," chills run down my back. I would never imagine those words would manifest in the Black Lives Matter Movement. But Satan saw the movement as an opportunity, and he disguised himself to lure the unsuspecting and undiscerning to bow down and worship him while aiding his advances.

Going back to Daniel 3, when King Nebuchadnezzar made a golden image, his intent was for all to bow and worship his golden statue. The first implicated in his schemes were his administration and all who held a rulership position within Babylon. Secondly, everyone else followed suit and bowed down, and worshiped the erected idol. However, those who knew and honored God refrained from bowing to King Nebuchadnezzar's idol.

Sadly, the scenario that took place with King Nebuchadnezzar is the same that has happened with the Black Lives Matter Movement. The first to bow down and worship the idol god of homosexuality were the ones who held a management office within the organization. Then, many government officials bowed the knee to this idol. And continuing the trickling effect, thousands of innocent civilians and affiliates of this organization have unknowingly bowed down to this hidden idol of homosexuality.

The spirit BLM has succumbed to is filled with disdain, hatred, rebellion, and spewed venom toward God our Creator. BLM has been engulfed by the prideful spirit of homosexuality. Anyone who joined forces with this movement (protests and all forms of support) has joined forces with this underlying demonic spirit. However, many believers received their revelation from God and realized this organization deceived them. They learned that Black Lives Matter did not have a genuine concern for black lives, but their hidden agenda was to advance homosexual rights. Sadly, their hidden agendas will destroy the nucleus and God's mandate for all, which is to be fruitful and multiply or, in other words, build a family and fulfill God's decree.

Although the women who founded the Black Lives Matter movement are filled with gall and bitterness, which resulted in Satan usurping their mission, many affiliated with their movement held pure intentions and simply fell victim and were led astray. However, I must mention that I would never undermine anyone's beliefs or passion for justice and, more specifically, righteous justice. I, too, am a black woman with two black sons and a black husband. I am furious with the injustice that has been dealt with to my kind. However, I am a huge advocate of righteousness, and I despise all that is evil. Therefore, I must speak out and play my position in exposing the evil and hidden agendas masked within organizations and missions that portray righteousness, proclaim good intention, and are supposed advocates for justice.

The solidarity stance of the bowing of the knee may be seen as an innocent move. However, for all believers involved in the ministry of deliverance, we know that the actions we take, no matter how innocent, are doorways or legal grounds for the devil to have access to our lives, our seeds, and in generations to come. Black Lives Matter is a vehicle for the idol of homosexuality. And where there are idols, there is witchcraft.

Recently, I was informed that the BLM Movement calls upon the spirit of dead ancestors. Therefore, I decided to investigate further to see if these claims were valid. I found the following article, "Black Lives Matter is Ushering in a New Religion," by Katelynn Richardson, August 22. I quote verbatim:

If the obsessive and unquestioning holding to social justice doctrine or pious bending of the knee in tribute to black lives all seemed faintly cultish to you, recent statements from black Lives Matter leaders confirm you were probably on the right track. "Spirituality is at the center of Black Lives Matter...If I did not do that, it would be antithetical to this work." Said BLM co-founder Patrisse Cullors in a June 13th conversation. This statement is not fake. Watch the discussion yourself. It is available on the Facebook page of the Fowler Museum at UCLA.

Melina Abdullah, professor of Pan-African studies at California State University and founder of BLM Los Angeles, responds to Cullors's statement with more insight into the spiritual nature of the movement. "We become very intimate with the spirits we call on," she says. What kind of spirits are they calling on? The dead, of course. When they ask you to say their name," it is not just an innocent way to honor their tragic loss of life. According to Cullors, they are chanting those names to summon their spirits. "When we speak their names, we invoke that spirit, and those spirits become present," she says.

Let me pause here for a moment. If you need to learn more, just google, and you will find it. As you read, you will get the sense that BLM is more than social justice. It is a movement infused with devils and idol worship of all sorts. Knowing that their basic practices are infused with this religion warns us not to take anything they say or do via social media, etc., lightly. Even the hashtags are a means of calling up spirits. So if you believe in Christ and have used their hashtag, merchandise, or the like, RENOUNCE, RENOUNCE, RENOUNCE!

Earlier I stated that Satan and his demons work undercover. All his activities are covert unless he is confronted. The only way he acts overtly is if his identity is uncovered, or he feels embolden by weakness, or he wants to intimidate through the display of pride. Satan is a deceiver. His goal is to deceive people into trusting him and not God. He portrays himself as a loving, caring being and depicts God as hateful, angry, strict, judgmental, and selfish, one who is not to be trusted. Satan uses his surrogates to portray himself as a beautiful, caring, compassionate person.

To further my claim, here is another excerpt from the same article written by Katelyn R:

> Hebah Farrag, assistant director of research at the USC Center for Religion and Civic Culture, writes this in an article for the Berkley Center:
> "The movement for Black lives works toward the goal of not just racial justice but freedom of the mind and the spirit. It encourages 'healing justice' so that people can heal from trauma and engage as the best version of themselves. The Movement infuses a syncretic blend of African and indigenous cultures, spiritual practices, and beliefs, embracing ancestor worship; Ifa-based rituals such as chanting, dancing, and summoning deities; and healing practices such as acupuncture, reiki, therapeutic massage, and plant medicine."

What more can I say? The premise of this book is to show that Satan's desire from the beginning is to be worship as the Most High God, and that has not changed. He desires to have all bow down to him, and he will do anything, use anyone, even unsuspecting saints, to obtain that worship. This book serves as a warning to the church. I am warning all against bowing down to Satan's agenda while encouraging everyone to test every spirit to see if they are from God. It is a warning not to walk according to our emotions but on the truth of God's Word.

Many of our brothers and sisters, including lay leaders, have latched on to the homosexual idol disguised as Black Lives Matter. They gave credence to this lying, deceiving, lewd spirit that was conjured up from the belly of hell. They have bowed down on their knees to this idol, which is confirmed in this article. BLM is about advancing the kingdom of darkness's agenda. They are not merely advocating for black men unjustly served by white police officers; they are about the homosexual agenda. According to ABC (digital) News, "From the start, Black Lives Matter has been about LGBTQ lives. It states that two of three Black Lives Matter founders identify as queer. From the beginning, the founders of Black Lives Matter have always put LGBTQ voices at the center of the conversation. The movement was founded by three Black women, Alicia Garza, Patrisse Cullors, and Opal Tometi, who identify as queer.

Update on Equality Act

It is here. Prepare to fight! February 27, 2021, has passed, and a new administration has been installed. I will not say voted in because that is questionable. There was an interruption of the quest to get what is known as the Equality Act. Of course, by the name, you probably can guess the cause: LGBTQ rights. This bill has passed the House and is now on its way to Senate.

For believers, this means, if passed in the senate, it will force Christians to bow down or bow out. Meaning, if we are Christian-based organizations, churches, etc., we must go against our religious convictions to accommodate the agenda of the LGBTQ or be persecuted. There is no exemption for religious beliefs in this bill. This bill, if passed, will set the stage for religious persecution in the United States. Now we must choose. As for me, for Christ I live, and for Christ I die. What about you? I encourage you, the reader, to find out the details of this bill. It is heinous.

Selah

I covered everything. After asking God how I should end this book, I sensed that after reading these articles, I should go no further and set forth a call to action. Everyone who has bowed their knees to this idol of homosexuality, BLM, or any other movements that promote the antichrist agenda, for that matter, God says you must repent. You must renounce your participation because you have bowed down your knee to none other than Satan! "**Repent and come out from them**, and I will forgive your sins and cleanse you from all unrighteousness," says the Lord (2 Cor. 6:17 and 1 John 1:9). Selah.

For the ones who did not bow down, the Lord your God commends you. Continue to stand. Do not bow down to fear or threats, nor any kind of intimidation. Fear not; the Lord, your God, is with you (Isaiah 41:10). God is not shaken; neither should you.

To the ones who bowed down, the Lord says, "I love you. Repent, renounce, and take a stand. Confess your sins, and I will restore you. Have no fellowship with the unfruitful works of darkness but rather expose them" (Eph. 5:11).

Prayer of Deliverance

Heavenly Father, I come to You in the merciful name of the Lord, Jesus my Lord and Savior. I renounce my affiliation with any movement, causes, and organizations that stand against Your Word. I repent of my participation by bowing my knees to them. I ask for Your forgiveness for my involvement in movements such as (say what they are)_____.

I stand today to sever my ties and agreement with Satan and his demons through my actions right now, in the mighty name of Jesus. I ask You to cleanse me and purify my bloodline. Set me and my lineage free from any claims Satan and his demons may have due to my actions. Heavenly Father, I thank You for hearing me and forgiving me. In the name of Jesus Christ, Your Son, Amen.

Reference Page

1. Chapter 3. – "Wile." Lexico.com, Accessed December 20, 2020, https://www.lexico.com/definition/wile.

2. Chapter 4 – Ben Arnoldy, "Erosion from Tahoe Fire May Hurt Lake's Health." The Christian Science Monitor, Published July 5, 2007,
   https://www.csmonitor.com/2007/0705/p02s01-usgn.html.

3. Chapter 4. – Tyler O'Neil, "Virginia Forces Christian Ministries to Adopt 'Government Ideology' or Pay $100K." PJ Media, Published September 30, 3020
   https://pjmedia.com/culture/tyler-o-neil/2020/09/30/virginia-forces-christian-ministries-to-adopt-government-ideology-or-pay-100k-n985842.

4. Chapter 4. – Ryan P. Burge, "The Pope Said He Supports Civil Unions for Same-Sex Couples. American Catholics Will Approve." The Washington Post, Published Oct. 23, 2020,
   https://www.washingtonpost.com/politics/2020/10/23/pope-said-he-supports-civil-unions-same-sex-couples-american-catholics-will-approve/.

5. Chapter 9. – Katelynn Richardson, "Black Lives Matter Is Ushering in a New Religion." Katelynn Richardson, Published August 22, 2020,

> https://katelynnrichardson.medium.com/blm-is-ushering-in-a-new-religion-d059a8fc1ede.

6. Chapter 9. – Sony Salzman, "From the Start, Black Lives Matter Has Been about LGBTQ Lives." ABC News, Published June 21, 2020,

> https://abcnews.go.com/US/start-black-lives-matter-lgbtq-lives/story?id=71320450.

www.ingramcontent.com/pod-product-compliance
Lightning Source LLC
LaVergne TN
LVHW051504070426
835507LV00022B/2922